The Art of Energy Healing

The Art of
Energy Healing

VOLUME ONE

The Foundation

SUSAN MATZ

BLUE DOLPHIN

Published by Blue Dolphin Publishing, Inc.
P.O. Box 8, Nevada City, CA 95959
Orders: 1-800-643-0765
Web: www.bluedolphinpublishing.com

ISBN: 1-57733-145-1

Library of Congress Cataloging-in-Publication Data

Matz, Susan D., 1965-
  The art of energy healing / Susan D. Matz.
    p. cm.
  ISBN 1-57733-145-1 (v. 1 : pbk. : alk. paper) — ISBN 1-57733-146-X (v. 2 :
pbk. : alk. paper)
  1. Energy—Therapeutic use. 2. Vital force—Therapeutic use. 3. Chakras—
Health aspects. I. Title.

RZ421.M38 2005
615.8'51—dc22

                                                      2005004575

Printed in the United States of America

10   9   8   7   6   5   4   3   2

*Dedicated to all of the Souls who are reaching out,
and all of the people who are reaching within.*

Contents

Preface

The information in this book is to help your mind grasp something that is not solid. It's very real, just not solid in the way the word is often thought of. If someone were studying to be a surgeon, they would have a physical body to work with. Something "solid" that the hands can touch, the eyes can see and the mind can easily grasp. Energy Healing is a form of self-discovery and change that honors, but does not always work with, something that can be physically touched. This asks that a person be open to other types of perception.

Many people learn information through the power of thought. The mind is heavily emphasized in this country, but there are other ways to absorb knowledge. Emotion, sound and creative expression are just a few examples of alternative ways to learn and grow. Another modality is *intuition*. Intuition is the ability to have direct knowledge about something without the mental process of comprehending through reasoning and rationalization.

People are generally used to processing information through a standard three-dimensional format, but some habits are definitely ready to be broken. People are multi-layered, multi-dimensional Beings. We are wonderfully complex with many layers, well beyond the basic three that most people are used to working with.

Energy Healing also deals with the fact that there is more to a person than the five known senses of smell/taste/hearing/touch/sight. Energy Healing encompasses things like the power of thought, emotion, feeling, intuition and spirituality.

Energy Healing is not about religion. It is about spirituality. Religion defines God. Spirituality is the concept of working with the essence of God without defining or confining God in a set of rules. Spirituality allows for each individual to define God through themselves, not through an outside set of concepts and rules.

Before a person can really work in Energy Healing, they have to be able to understand who they are as an individual. *You can Know another Human Being only to the degree that you can Know yourself.* Self-exploration is the journey of any true healer and every person who seeks to be healed.

This is a two-book series. Volume I is an introduction to the levels of consciousness, the Energy System and general content related to Energy Healing. Volume II is a more in-depth explanation of what is introduced in Volume I as well as information on spiritual concepts and healing techniques. The information in both of these books is my perception of the healing process. In both Volumes, the focus is more on understanding your False Self than your True Self. This is because everyone's Truth is individual. Once you peel away the layers of what is false, you'll find your own Truth.

A healer is born from within. In order for anyone's inner healer to emerge, self-exploration and training are part of the process. Healers aren't "special" or "gifted" people. They're just people, people who looked within and found out more about themselves than they could have ever understood with just their minds.

Here's to your inner healer emerging.

Susan D. Matz

CHAPTER ONE

Energy Healing

Energy Healing is where science, medicine and spirituality all come together. Science works with molecular structure, medicine works with understanding and healing the physical body, and spirituality works with the power of God. Energy Healing combines all three of these components.

From a scientific standpoint, every substance is created from *matter*. Matter is created by molecular structures. Molecular structures can be broken down into molecules, and molecules can be broken down into atoms. Atoms themselves can be broken down into something smaller, but, to date, science has not been able to break down an atom far enough to discover what it's actually made of. In other words, science has not yet found the source that creates all life. There are so many different theories in science, but one thing science can agree on is that when broken down, everything is pure energy.

Medicine sees the human body as a powerful, complex machine. Though much has been learned about the human body, there is still so much that medicine cannot explain. The term "doctor" has been around for a few thousand years but it has been loosely used. Formal medical schools did not come into play until the late 1700s in Europe and the 1800s in the U.S., but even then, in the U.S. a "medical" school in the early 1900s could have meant anything. Usually it meant chiropractic medicine (and not the chiropractic medicine of today.) It wasn't until the mid-1900s that medical schools became a little more regulated and formalized. It's been a rocky road for Western medicine but a very impressive one. When science and

1

medicine came together, wonderful things happened, from the creation of pharmaceuticals to high-tech machinery that helps save lives on a daily basis in today's hospitals.

When translated, the word "healing" means *whole*. This is exactly what healers work with, the *whole* person. Science works with the technicality, medicine works with the physicality, and Energy Healing deals with both, adding the element of spirituality. Healing is the definitive of the Mind-Body-Spirit connection. It is in the work of Energy Healing that all three are brought together.

Healers have been around for millions of years. Eastern cultures are the most prominent in having documented energetic pathways in the body for many centuries. The most commonly documented Eastern healing technique is Acupuncture. This is the art of placing very small needles directly into the energy pathways of a body in order to affect physical healing or to change an unhealthy pattern such as smoking. Energy Healing works with these same pathways, but uses both the client and the healer's energy instead of acupuncture needles.

Energy Healing is another thread in our evolution. It is not meant to compete with medicine or science. It's meant to add on. Initially medicine and science were two separate fields of study that did not necessarily see eye-to-eye with each other, but eventually they came together in a wonderfully symbiotic relationship. Energy Healing is just another layer to weave into this relationship. It adds spirituality into the mix. Science may not be able to prove what is the source of all cellular matter, all life, but healers don't need that proof. Energy Healing works outside of the five basic senses and does not rely on standard scientific elements to prove its existence. Energy Healing works on the concept that if you could break down the atom far enough you would find that everything is created from spirit, more specifically God. Not "God" in the traditional 'fire and brimstone' religious connotation, but God as defined in terms of pure energy. God is called the "Creator" because God is pure creative energy. This means that everything—a chair, a window, a book, a pencil, a dog and a human being—are all made out of the same energetic substance. If science were able to break everything down to its most basic component, it would find that all energy is created from the same source. In Energy Healing, this source is defined as God.

Energy Healing is not a religious debate. It's not about religion at all, but rather *spirituality*. For people who are drawn to healing (whether as the healer or the client) there really is no question that God runs through everything. If someone is still questioning this concept, then they are generally not drawn to see a healer. They probably won't be reading this book! When people hear the word "God," it often kicks in pre-prejudicial religious teachings. The real definition of God is not found in a church, a book or a classroom, it is found in your heart. This may sound hokey, but it's so true. Part of a healer's job is to help a client connect into their heart. It's at this level that the mind of Man meets the spirit of God. When this happens, each person can define "God" in their own way. A healer is not some spiritual guru (and if you run across one that says they are, you just might want to keep running!). And a healer is not there to tell you who and what you are. A healer's job is to help you find out who you really are and let you define it for yourself. A true healer is a guide, not a dictator, and not someone running around claiming they have all your answers.

Traditionally, medicine focuses on diagnosing and curing illness. Medical science tends to see a disease as "the enemy" that needs to be killed. Energy Healing takes a different perspective because it sees illness/injury as the result of blocked energy in the physical body. The blocked areas are trying to get a message across to the person. "Listen to your body" is a very literal term in Energy Healing. An energy healer helps a client to connect and communicate with their own body so they can find that message.

The physical body is surrounded by an Energy Field also known as the *aura*. The Energy Field has seven layers to it, the first layer actually attaching into the physical body. The physical body is an amazing thing, but it is limited in how much information it can process on its own. The body is like a machine and tends to understand things in primitive ways like "have cut, send white cells for healing." On its own, the body does not see the cut as anything more than a tear that needs repairing.

Many studies have been done on the effectiveness of placebos, and though the studies differ in why they think the placebos work, they do show that they work. Placebos are essentially fake pills (usually made of sugar) that are given to a patient instead of a real medication with nothing more than the suggestion that the pill will make them better. When the person swallows the pill, it goes through the digestive tract. The liver recognizes that the "pill" is just sugar, so why does it work?

The Energy Field adds the power of beliefs, spirituality and emotion into the mix. So whatever a person believes at the time they take the "pill," their Energy Field absorbs this into the physical body and adds it to the many messages the liver is already receiving. The physical body may tell the liver "this is pure sugar," but let's says in this scenario, the person has a strong spiritual conviction and believes that God is taking care of them by lowering their blood pressure through this "pill." The person's spiritual belief gets sent to the liver through the Energy Field where the liver adds it to all of the other messages it's getting. The liver then says, "Okay, let's send this pill along with the message that the blood pressure is to be lowered"— even though the liver understands that biologically the "pill" is merely compressed sugar.

There are seven specific areas in the body where the Energy Field communicates directly with the physical body through something called a *chakra*. Inside a person's physical body messages are sent through two main paths, the nervous system (which consists of your brain and spinal column) and the endocrine system (which regulates hormonal activity.) Both hormones and nerve endings give and receive tens of thousands of messages inside the body each day. They're basically the human e-mail service. The Chakra System, which consists of seven different chakras, is the pathway that gives and receives messages between the Energy Field and the physical body. It's the human brain that regulates the whole process. Information traveling inside your physical body is like having local e-mail service, and the Chakra System represents global e-mail service because it sends messages in and out of the body.

Your physical body is the only part of you limited to being three-dimensional. Your Energy Field consists of many more dimensions and sees life as having far more depth and meaning than just what appears on the surface. It's at a level beyond the third dimension that illness/injury is seen as a message sent to help a person have a more in-depth understanding of both themselves and the life they are living. The focus in Energy Healing is not to "cure" a disease but rather to heal it. Healing deals with exploring and understanding *why* someone gets sick to begin with and what that illness/injury is trying to help them understand about themselves. Healing works with the concept that nothing is random or an accident, that every event and illness in a person's life has a deeper meaning behind it. And everyone's meaning is unique to them. In other words, ten people diagnosed with the same type of diabetes will have ten different reasons behind why they developed diabetes. This is very different from traditional medicine which is built on categorizing all disease and injury into systematic modalities of treatment.

Energy Healing is not an exploration process that works by categorizing illness, or developing routine treatment plans. It is never the illness/injury that is the focus, but rather the person as a whole. What is that person's spirit trying to get across to them? What is the bigger picture that created the illness/injury to begin with? Healing is not about curing, it is about evolving.

By the time someone is drawn to a reputable healer they are at a point in their personal growth where they want to understand themselves at a deeper level and are willing to see things about themselves (and their behavior) at a deeper level. There are plenty of unskilled, disreputable healers out there more than willing to tell a person they can "cure" anything for the right amount of money. But remember, there are just as many disreputable doctors out there willing to do things like write prescriptions for patients they've never even examined. Like anything in life, the more willing you are to take self-responsibility, the better choices you will make, like picking a good healer.

True healing is not a quick fix. Healing requires that a client actively participate in their own process. The client has to be willing to look within and allow change to happen. When someone enters the journey that is Energy Healing, their life will change. You cannot possibly look deep within and not have your outer reality shift.

This is probably the biggest hurdle most people have to overcome. Often when a client starts seeing a healer, they are motivated to either heal a physical illness/injury or change their life in some way, like stopping a pattern of abusive relationships. Part of the client wants this change, or they wouldn't pay good money to see a healer if they didn't. But there is usually another part that is terrified of change, even if it means being completely healed of a serious illness. The part that doesn't want to change has underlying motivations for staying ill or staying in a negative behavioral pattern. For most people, this part of their nature is unconscious. Everyone has a dark side to their psyche. This is why it is important to understand how your consciousness works when embarking on any spiritual or healing process. Anyone can read something in a book or learn something in a classroom, but it doesn't mean that they really understand the true meaning of what they were taught. I have met many people who could expound on things like God, healing or chakras. They could quote book after book *but they weren't living what they were preaching.* "Practice what you preach" is a very old saying and goes right along with "walk the talk." I don't know who coined these phrases but they are wonderfully said. Just because your mind can mimic something doesn't mean you understand it.

You are not just your mind. Your mind is only a fraction of who you are. The study of Anatomy and Physiology divides the human body up into eleven separate areas called *systems*, like the digestive system, the respiratory system and the cardiovascular system. The nervous system, which includes the brain, is only one of the eleven systems. The brain itself is only about 3% of the body. Most people over-identify with the power of thought. Granted, thoughts are powerful, but not as powerful as you might believe them to be. There are many ways to take in and process information; mental thought is actually a small percentage of how the body functions.

Healing is a journey into areas of yourself that have always been there, and most likely control your life on a daily basis. These are areas that your consciousness is just not aware of yet. Energy Healing is not about finding a problem and "fixing" it. Energy Healing is about self-exploration, self-discovery, change, growth and empowerment. When any illness is truly healed, it is the end result of someone opening up an area within them that had previously been locked away. A cure is temporary at best. Because whatever was cured will just come back either in the same exact form, like a returning tumor, or in another form that is just as serious and just as determined to get its message heard.

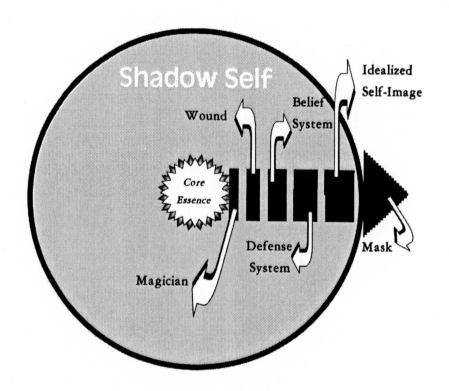

THE SHADOW SELF

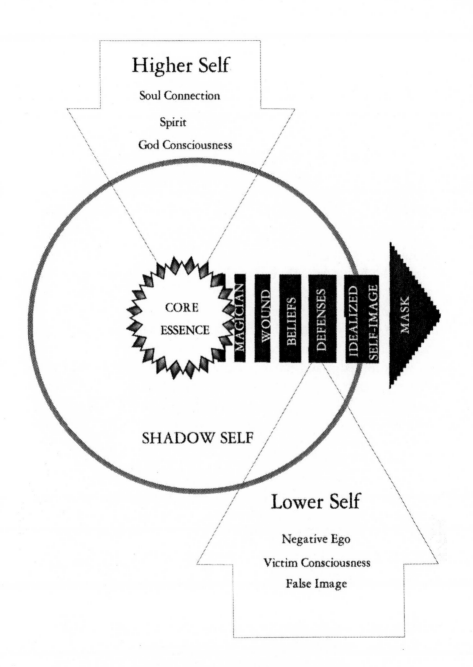

HIGHER SELF / LOWER SELF

CHAPTER TWO

To Know Thy Self

When a person is first born, they have a direct connection to their spirit. There is a line of energy that connects the physical body to the spiritual body like an umbilical cord, only this one does not get cut at birth. As each day goes by this spiritual connection becomes more and more like a distant memory. When the mind starts to develop, it begins to identify more with the physical world a person is born into than their spiritual connection. The mind becomes filled with learned knowledge and starts to close off the pathways in the brain that are connected to Knowing. *Knowing* is what comes from spirit. Learned knowledge comes from Man, and though it can have Truth in it, much of the knowledge that comes through the mind of Man is usually coated with negative ego and fear.

From birth each person is divided. There is the part of you that is, and always will be, connected to your spirit. This is your *light.* When you are in your light, you are in your True Self. Then there is the part of you that becomes attached to what goes on in this world, both what you are told to believe in and what you learn on your own, but this part of you is disconnected from your spirit. This is your *dark.* When you are in your dark, you are in your False Self. When something is dark, it does not always mean that it's "evil." Darkness is simply the absence of light. The more light that is missing the darker something is. In Energy Healing, the goal is to help a person identify their dark areas as well as their light areas.

Anything you learn that does not come from light is *false.* Many parents and teachers pass along information that is inaccurate because they are merely teaching something that was taught to them (or done to them) without having the experience of connecting into their own light to discern if what they were taught was really the Truth. This is how many dark things have been perpetuated on this planet. It doesn't necessarily mean that there were consciously bad intentions behind what you were taught. It just means that what you were taught may not have been Truth. Remember, at one time children grew up being taught that the world was flat. Nothing evil there, just ignorance that led to perpetuating a falsehood. Each new generation that is born struggles to bring more light, more Truth, into the world.

Finding your own Truth becomes very significant when studying religion or spirituality. Everyone has their own opinion about God. Everyone has their own definition of a "good person" versus a "bad person." There are millions of different opinions. The only time you will ever really Know all the answers to life's big questions is when you are connected to *your* True Self. Until then, all you're doing is taking on someone else's opinion. A healer's job is not to define "spirit" or "God" for anyone, but it is to help a person connect into their True Self so that they can find their own answers.

Energetically, the part in you that Knows truth is called your Core Essence. This is the area in you that is always in the light. It is always connected to your spirit and God. The part in you that does not function from Truth is your Shadow Self. The Shadow Self consists of all the areas in your conscious and unconsciousness that are not in the light. When you look at these areas intuitively, they actually look dark, hence the name Shadow Self.

The Core Essence is made up of several layers. These consist of your Higher Self, your soul, your soul family, soul group, guides, spiritual guardian and of course, God. Though it may not seem so at times, you are never abandoned from light. Your Core Essence is always connected to you, always within you. You are never alone. What happens is that a person's conscious mind slowly forgets about their Core Essence starting from the moment they're born. The more a person forgets, the more lost they feel in life. "Who am I?" and "What is my purpose in life?" are very common questions from people who are feeling lost in this world. Traditionally, certain cultures raised their children with the intention of helping them to remember their Essence by teaching about spirit and spiritual guides starting from the day they are born. Most people today are not raised to remember their light. They are raised to conform to society.

Energetically your consciousness has seven basic layers. Six of the layers sit in the Shadow Self and the seventh layer is the connection into your Core Essence. The six layers of the Shadow are the Mask, Idealized Self-Image, Defense System, Belief System, Wound and Magician. Each will be explained in more depth.

The Shadow Self was created by the *negative ego*. "Ego" is another word for personality. In traditional psychoanalysis, a person's personality is divided into three sections known as the id, ego and superego. The 'id' represents primitive instincts, the 'superego' is morality (this is all of the ethical training you learned from your family and society while growing up.) In traditional therapy, the ego sits between the id and the superego to mediate your primal instincts with your socialization. In Energy Healing the word ego is used to represent *all* aspects of your personality. The negative ego is the part of your personality that comes from the Shadow and is called the **Lower Self**. When the personality comes from the Core Essence it is known as the **Higher Self**. The more a person is willing to acknowledge and work with their Shadow Self, the more energy they will dissolve out of the Shadow and bring back into their Core Essence. Then their personality will stem more from their Higher Self than the self-serving Lower Self. People who have a strong connection to their Core Essence have a gentle and loving personality simply because the majority of their personality is radiating from their Higher Self.

Everyone is born with the same amount of energy. No one person has more or less energy than another. Someone who is deeply connected to their Core Essence has more of their energy *in* their Core Essence, which does not mean that they have more energy. In other words the Dalai Lama, for example, does not have any more energy than you; he just has more of his energy connected to his Core Essence. This can be a hard concept to accept because the Lower Self would like you to believe that "spiritual people" are different because they have more "spiritual energy" than the average person. This is not true, energy is energy. It is simply a matter of where that energy is coming from that makes such a big difference. There are only twenty-four hours in a day; no matter how you divide up the day the end result is twenty-four hours. It is the same principle with a person's energy: each person is born with the same amount of energy; it may be divided up into different areas for different people *but the overall amount of energy is exactly the same.*

The majority of people gradually disconnect more and more energy from their Core Essence as they grow up. They give that energy over to their Shadow Self (usually because this is what society and parental pressure dictates) which increases a person's amount of dark energy and decreases their amount of light energy. You could be as connected to your Core Essence as any Spiritual Master. Everyone has the same potential, so it's just a matter of how much work you put into the process.

Remember, darkness is not always evil; "darkness" refers to the areas in you that are not fully connected to light. **Light is always in Truth, unconditional and loving**. The Lower Self is not dumb. It has the capacity to learn and imitate anything it wants. What it wants most is to imitate the Higher Self so that it can fool you into believing that what you think is coming from light is actually coming from darkness. In a way, it is like there is a war going on inside of everyone. You only have so much energy; you can't get any more, so in order for the Lower Self to be in power it has to get the energy out of the Core Essence and into the Shadow Self. In other words it has to get energy out of the Higher Self in order to increase the amount of energy circulating in the Lower Self. It's kind of like a game where whoever has the most pieces wins except in this case the "pieces" are your energy and whoever has the most "pieces" of your energy gets to be in control of you and your life. If the majority of your energy is stuck in the Lower Self, then that's where you function from; however if the majority of your energy is in your Higher Self, then that's where you will live from.

If God was given the title of "boss" over the Core Essence, then it would be the negative ego that would be given the title of "boss" over the Shadow Self. God has the advantage because, when you are born, your consciousness is connected to God, so your consciousness is always in your Higher Self. The negative ego has to work at getting energy into your Lower Self. It usually does this by fooling your consciousness into believing that something is unconditional, loving and in truth when it is not. In other words, it tries to make the dark look good. The more your actions and choices come from darkness, the more energy you give over to your Lower Self, taking that very energy away from your Higher Self.

For example, Sally F. is the friend that is always there when anyone is in crisis. She gives and gives all the time. If you just look at outside appearances, you can be fooled into believing that Sally F. is working from the light. But she is not; she is actually working from the dark because her *underlying motivation* is manipulative. Sally F. gives and gives but then she wants people to give back to her. She has an underlying motivation that says 'I give to you now, you give to me later.' In other words her "acts of kindness" have strings attached to them; they are conditional. She is trying to get her personal needs met by manipulating others. This is an example of the negative ego trying to look like the Core Essence by doing "kind" acts when those acts are really for a dark purpose. This goes back to the basic concept of "don't judge a book by its cover"; read a few pages and see what it's really about versus believing something just because on the surface it looks good.

When someone is coming from darkness, it is not always as obvious as a blatant lie, stealing or one person killing another. It takes a lot of honest, self-discovery for a person to identify and acknowledge the aspects of their nature that originate from their Shadow Self. It is unlikely that you are as bad, or as good, as your conscious mind leads you to believe.

As people, we really do create our own reality; it's just that the majority of the time most people are in their Lower Self so the majority of time most people are creating their lives from darkness. Ignorance is never "bliss," it only perpetuates darkness. The world will not change by forcing change to come from the outside. The world simply reflects the energy of the people living in that world. Real change evolves one person at a time. The more each person learns to come from their Core Essence, their light, the more the planet itself will be in light.

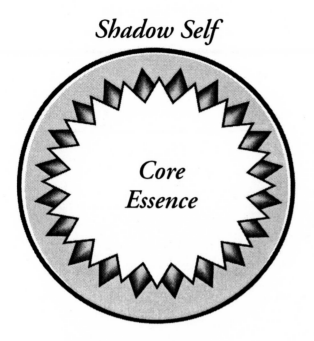

Shadow Self

Core Essence

Average relationship between the *Core Essence* and the *Shadow Self* of a 2-month-old healthy infant.

GROWTH PROCESS OF THE SHADOW SELF

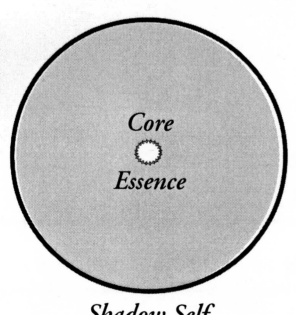

Core

Essence

Shadow Self

Average relationship between the *Core Essence* and the *Shadow Self* of a 30-year-old healthy adult.

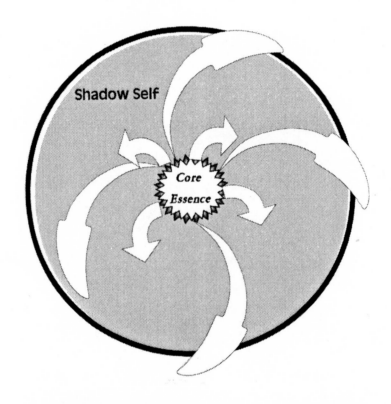

Shadow Self

Core
Essence

Each time a person dissolves an aspect of their *Shadow Self*, the *Core Essence* comes shining through, bringing with it their unique soul qualities. This is what it means to express your "soul's desire." In order to live from your soul, you first have to let it out!

CHAPTER THREE

The Conscious, the Unconscious and Awareness

The "layers" of the Shadow Self are not actually physical layers that you can touch with your hand. These are layers of consciousness and cannot necessarily be felt by physically touching them, but they can be reached by your *awareness*. There is a difference between being *aware* and being conscious. When you have a conscious thought, it simply means that your mind, which is often controlled by your negative ego, is allowing you to perceive something. That "something" does not always have to be Truth; it can be anything that the negative ego wants you to believe as being the truth. When you are in awareness, you perceive more than just what your mind is telling you. Awareness connects you to multiple levels of perception which allows you to get information in more ways than just through the power of thought. Awareness is always connected to a person's Core Essence, so the more energy a person has coming from their Core Essence, the more awareness a person has. Awareness leads to true Knowing.

When a baby is born, it has a lot of awareness but not a lot of consciousness. Consciousness requires thought, and a newborn baby does not have the capacity for thinking. Thought is something that develops each day a baby gets older. In developmental growth, the ability to think comes before the ability to speak. There is a reason

17

newborns don't talk; they don't know how! If a newborn baby could talk, it could tell you more about what goes on inside a Newborn Nursery than the adults working there. This is because a newborn is still so connected to their Core Essence that they have a very broad awareness of what is really going on. Their mind is just not developed enough to translate the information they are getting into words.

Some examples of what newborns can be aware of are the emotions of everyone in the nursery, adults as well as babies. They're aware of the stories behind each of the babies, what their parents are like and the soul purpose as to why each baby was paired with their particular parent(s). They're aware of the physical sensations of everyone in the nursery. They are aware of the physical sensations of each adult in the room better than the adults themselves because most adults have a low level of awareness when it comes to what their physical bodies are feeling. How many times have you had a cut but did not remember where or when you got the cut? How often have you come home from work and suddenly felt exhausted or took a quick break and realized how sore your body was? Your body is feeling everything that happens to it all the time, but your negative ego only lets you become conscious of what your body **is already feeling** when it decides to let you feel your own body. The degree that a person is numb to their physical body is another indicator of how disconnected their consciousness is from their Core Essence.

To become *consciously aware* means that your consciousness is being fed information from your Core Essence and not your negative ego. You are always conscious on some level, but the more awareness you let into your conscious mind, the more you are *consciously aware* of what is **really** going on around (and within) you at all times. Just because someone is "conscious" of something does not mean that they really know what is going on. They can simply be conscious of what another person, a book, the media or their own negative ego tells them to believe. Most people are usually only conscious of what they want to be conscious of. A person has to have awareness to see what is really happening, otherwise, they are just seeing what they want to see.

Your True Self never avoids, it never just looks at the "pretty" stuff. It is willing to see everything and be in full awareness of everything. **You can only change that which you are willing to be aware of.** If you are unwilling to be aware of Truth, then you cannot be fully connected to your Core Essence. It is the negative ego that wants to avoid Truth so that it can continue to rule your consciousness. So it can continue to rule you! Your negative ego is very selective about what it wants you to see. For example, if you smoke, then whenever an advertisement comes on television that talks about how unhealthy smoking is, your negative ego will lower your consciousness level so that you won't have to fully acknowledge the advertisement. In other words it kind of zones you out for a few minutes. The more a person is willing to see Truth, the less power their negative ego has over them.

You can see the significance of connecting to your awareness. Awareness increases your level of truly understanding yourself and the world around you. Your answers are never going to be found outside of you; they are always within your Core Essence. It is here that you will find all the gifts you already have and all the ones you are learning to develop.

Most people don't know what they Know. They are *unconscious*. When someone is unconscious, it does not mean that the information isn't there, it just means that you are not aware of the information. Your Core Essence is always connected to you; it's just a matter of how connected you are to your Core Essence! So *unconsciousness* is the space where your conscious self does not connect to your awareness.

Whereas traditional psychotherapy works with the concept of id, ego and superego, Energy Healing works with the three levels of consciousness, unconsciousness and awareness. Energy Healing is not analysis. It is part of a healer's job to explain what is going on, but the explanation is there to help bring *conscious awareness* to the unconscious aspects of a client. A healing is really about increasing awareness and shifting energy from the Lower Self back into the Higher Self where it originated.

Everyone's Shadow Self looks unique, just as everyone on the planet is unique. As a person grows and learns, their Shadow will shift and change. The basic model (see illustrations) representing the Shadow Self is based on the levels of conscious awareness in a person's

Energy Field. The model was drawn to represent each level of the Shadow Self in its relationship to the Core Essence. In reality, people will have different amounts of energy in different sections. For example, some people will have a lot of energy in their Wound, others in their Idealized Self-Image. An exercise in self-exploration is to draw your own Shadow Self. Just let your hand relax and place the dividing lines wherever it wants to. This is a way to help you discover where your energy is being held. This is also an exercise in allowing more awareness to flow through you.

In general, people who are oblivious to their spiritual selves have a large and dark Shadow. People who are more spiritually connected (this means a real spiritual connection and not one of those spiritual quick-fixes) have a much smaller Shadow Self and a larger Core Essence.

You can't change something about yourself until you stop and own where you are right now. Exploring where your energy is in regards to your Shadow Self and Core Essence is not about judging yourself, but rather about understanding yourself. How and why you do what you do, who you really are. Acknowledging and exploring your Shadow Self is about acknowledging and exploring your True Self. This process is about honoring all of your experiences so you can let go of the ones that no longer serve you and expand the ones that do serve you. It is your choice as to how much awareness you are going to let into your conscious mind. The more Truth you allow yourself to know, the more empowerment you will have. Real empowerment always comes from the Core Essence. Empowerment is never about controlling yourself or other people. Empowerment is the ability to make healthy choices. The more awareness a person has, the healthier choices they make. Healthier choices lead to happier lives.

Shadow Self of a 32-year-old salesman

Shadow Self of a 52-year-old woman who was sexually abused as a small child

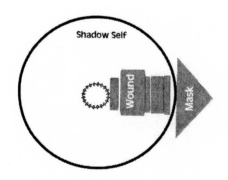

Shadow Self of a 20-year-old person diagnosed with Schizophrenia

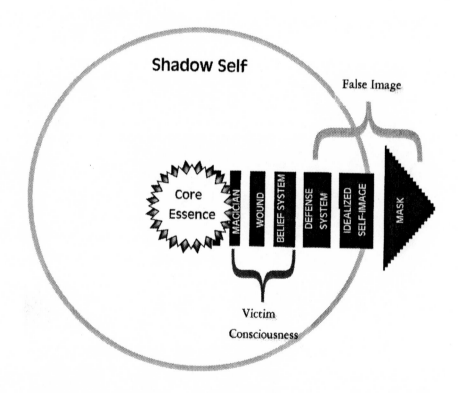

Shadow Self

False Image

Core Essence

MAGICIAN

WOUND

BELIEF SYSTEM

DEFENSE SYSTEM

IDEALIZED SELF-IMAGE

MASK

Victim Consciousness

VICTIM CONSCIOUSNESS / FALSE IMAGE

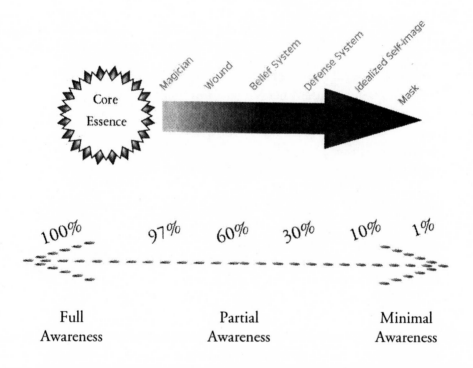

LEVELS OF AWARENESS

CHAPTER FOUR

The Shadow Self

The flow of all energy originates from inside the Core Essence. Energy flows out to the Energy Field and then back into the Core Essence. It's a gentle back and forth movement that is in constant motion. The six layers of the Shadow represent the six layers of **consciousness** that your energy goes through. The Magician is the first layer in the Shadow and represents the place where your consciousness first realizes it is an individual. The next layer is the Wound where all of your real (and perceived) traumas are held. The Belief System follows and holds all of the statements and individual beliefs that you took on from places like your family and society. A Defense System sits in the middle and it's how the Shadow Self deals with fear. Whenever the conscious mind does not remember that it is one with God, it becomes fearful of things like failure, pain or death, and this is when the Defense System is called in. (Whenever your consciousness *is* connected to God, it understands that there is no "death" only re-births, and that you cannot possibly fail because everything you do, you do for the experience and not the outcome.) The next level is the Idealized Self-Image, what most people probably think of as the "ego" because it's at this level that your consciousness has an over-inflated concept of who you really are. It "idealizes" your self-image. The last level is the Mask and it is at this level that the negative ego convinces your conscious mind of what you should or should not be aware of.

The farther away your conscious mind is from the Core Essence, the less awareness you have of what is really Truth. The outer three layers of the Shadow represent a person's *False Image*. If there is a lot of energy trapped in someone's False Image, they are less likely to explore themselves. If they do wind up in traditional therapy or go to a healer, they generally go to appease a spouse or they spend the session time projecting their issues onto other people. The False Image avoids taking self-responsibility, and it avoids acknowledging that a person creates their own problems. When a person is in their False Image, they struggle against owning the consequences of their actions. It is hard for someone in their False Image to acknowledge their issues because this level of consciousness is so far removed from the Core Essence.

The inner three layers of the Shadow make-up a person's *Victim Consciousness*. At this level a person has no problem acknowledging their issues, but they struggle to let go of them. They use their issues as a crutch and create a victim-oriented mentality. "I can't" and "nobody understands me" are the theme songs for this part of the Shadow.

The negative ego uses both the Victim Consciousness and False Image to trap energy inside the Shadow Self. Healing is not just about connecting to your Core Essence, it is about owning your Shadow Self. It is *your* energy trapped in the Shadow, and it is only when you explore and own every part of your Shadow that you can be whole again. The following is a more in-depth explanation of each level in the Shadow. The more you can acknowledge your Shadow, and how much energy you have in each layer, the closer you are to dissolving that Shadow.

Statements of:
The Magician

"I am God"

"Your life is in my control"

"I know everything"

"I decide what you will or will not do. I will not let you forget this"

"I will show you all that you need to know. Don't listen to them"

"I am the only One who has always been there for you"

"You do not need to work on yourself, you're already perfect"

"Without me you do not exist"

"You will suffer and die without my guidance"

"Actually I'm better than God because I've never left you"

"I am everything"

"I will guide you to all that is good"

CHAPTER FIVE

Magician

The Magician is the first level to separate from the Core Essence and develop its own consciousness. It is the foundation of the Shadow Self. It is also the most intelligent and versatile part of the Shadow. The Magician has a direct *awareness* of the Core Essence. This is the only part of the Shadow that knows it evolved out of the Core Essence. The other five levels of the Shadow have a vague sense of the Core Essence but they do not have the direct connection that the Magician does.

The vast majority of people have some knowledge of God. It might be based on religion, family beliefs or personal beliefs, but wherever it comes from, it is learned. Not remembered. Since the Magician has a direct connection to the Core Essence, it is the only aspect of the Shadow that has a direct *awareness* that it is part of God.

This places the Magician in competition with God for what it perceives as control over your consciousness. The Magician does not want you aware that you are part of God because then you would look to God for support. As it stands, the Magician is the sole supporter of the Shadow Self and the Shadow Self is your present state of consciousness. This means that your mind can believe that there is a God, but when your energy seeks out this God, it gets stopped by the Magician. The Magician will appear God-like but in the more biblical sense, meaning it will act as an authoritarian God telling your energy what it should do and how it should behave.

If your energy was able to make it back to your Core Essence, it would find support in a very different way as God is not an authori-

27

tarian. God works with compassion and love to help support you in what you are truly seeking.

This is an important distinction because often what a person wants is not what they are truly seeking on a soul level. A person's desire frequently gets caught up in their unfulfilled wounds. An example of this is a woman who grew up in a household where she experienced verbal and emotional abuse from her mother every day. As a little girl there was a part of her that looked to her daddy to "rescue" her, but the father never stopped the mother's abusive behavior. As an adult, instead of allowing herself to see that her father enabled the mother and failed to protect her, she puts him up on a pedestal and tells everyone that her father was the "best." This is her way of avoiding her painful childhood experiences. Then she prays to God to "send me someone as great as my daddy." God would not send her someone as passively abusive as her father; He would send her someone that would love and support her in a healthy way.

The Magician, however, is more than willing to fulfill the desire of her consciousness. The problem is that most of a person's consciousness is distorted in their Shadow Self. This is why much of what a person initially desires is actually unhealthy for them. If they look deeper within and connect to their Core Essence, they will find Truth. It is only when a person is in Truth that their desires come from a healthier place.

As in the above example, the Magician will bring someone forth who is similar to her father and she will have just as miserable a time in that relationship as she did when she was a child living at home with her parents.

The Magician is very reactionary and just wants to give you what will make you happy in the moment. It wants you to be instantaneously happy so that you don't look any deeper within yourself. It is like giving a child food every time they cry, or putting them in front of the TV if they are bored. It's a quick fix that makes them forget what the problem was to begin with. It numbs them out.

When looking for God, religions do this frequently. Many religions have a rather simplistic ritual, sometimes even a mere statement like "I forsake all in the name of God," and then all past hurts and sorrows are supposedly absolved. This is similar to the

Magician who wants you to believe that God is just a breath away, that you don't have to take responsibility for all you have said and done to be fully connected to God. In other words it says, don't look at your Shadow Self, just go to God. Of course it would say this because, if you looked at past and present behaviors, then you would discover your darker nature which might encourage you to change! If you just "go to God," *chances are you will wind up at the level of the Magician* who spends a lot of time impersonating God. When you experience the real energy of God, you will never be fooled by your Magician again—they couldn't be more different.

People connect to God all the time in prayer and meditation. But if you leave your Shadow Self behind, then you are leaving a very large part of yourself behind when you connect to God. Often when people meditate or pray, they are looking only to connect to all that is good or light within themselves and the universe—they deny their Shadow Self. Bringing all that you are, good and not so good, into prayer and meditation will bring you not only closer to God but closer to loving and accepting yourself unconditionally. God does not expect you to be perfect; He loves you as you are now. The more of your Shadow Self that you work through, the more of your consciousness becomes *aware* of God. Then you go from *believing* that you're a part of God, to *Knowing* that you are part of God.

In the Shadow Self, the Magician has the most to lose if you were to connect to your Core Essence and God. This makes the Magician the most challenging part of your negative ego. In order to dissolve the Magician, you have to be able to surrender to your Core Essence. You have to be able to look deeply at your desires and let go of them if they serve some part of your Shadow Self. It is only that which is in your highest interest that God will serve. This process takes self-discovery and rarely, if ever, happens overnight.

As you journey through your own unconscious and conscious existence, the Magician will try and meet all the desires of your Shadow Self. You have to be willing to realize that most of your desires are unhealthy. You have to be willing to be uncomfortable in yourself for a little while. This is because **your Magician helps you to be comfortable in your darkness, so when you initially start living from your light, it is often uncomfortable.** Part of what makes it uncomfortable is that you have to go through the process of acknowl-edging that some of the misery in your life was there because you chose a quick fix instead of looking deeper within yourself. This is not about judging yourself, but about living from a deeper place of self-honesty and Truth.

There is an irony in today's world. We have never been so spiritually open, and yet we have never been so obsessed with instantaneous gratification. One negates the other. The Magician will offer that gratification, but it is not real. It will come with defeat, ignorance, abuse, depression, lack of personal power, life without joy or connection to what is REAL. God will offer Truth. Which do you choose?

CHAPTER SIX

Wound

At the level of the Wound, energy is trapped in clusters. Energy is in a "cluster" when the energetic particles are held together in a group, like a bunch of grapes, instead of being in their natural state which is flowing. When energy is in a cluster, it is *trapped energy*. An example of trapped energy would be watching a gently flowing stream, then looking down and seeing areas of water trapped by rock formations. The rocks hold in the water and keep it from flowing with the rest of the stream. The stream represents energy flowing and the small pools of trapped water represent energy clusters.

The consciousness of the Wound filters all of your life's experiences and chooses which experiences it believes to be painful. When the Wound decides that a particular experience is painful, it takes all of the energy related to that experience and proceeds to trap the energy and hold it in your Energy Field. The Wound believes that, if it holds onto your "hurt" energy, you won't have to actually feel the pain of the experience. It's a bit like stuffing a bill you don't want to deal with at the back of the pile. But as most people know, that which you ignore, hide or stuff away comes back to haunt you.

You cannot avoid pain, and the act of avoidance itself causes more pain. Whether you deal with your issues or not, they're still there. The more you avoid dealing with your pain, the bigger it gets. For example, Karen F. is in marriage where she is emotionally abused but she doesn't fully acknowledge the abuse. This is typical of what the Wound does: it keeps stuffing the pain away in hopes that everything will just get better one day. Well it won't; life only "gets better" when you deal with the issues in life that are causing you pain. In this example, Karen F. waits five years until she finally gets divorced. Now she has the added pain of shame to deal with because she created shame within herself over the fact that she allowed the abuse to go on for five years before she walked away.

Because energy clusters are trapped, they re-live each perceived "hurt" over and over again as if it is still happening. This is known as *cycling*. It isn't until the energy is released that it can let go of the painful experience. If you throw your dirty laundry in the closet and close the door, it will remain dirty until the day you take it out and clean it. It won't just go away; you have to take it out of the closet and deal with it. When a person is cycling, they will recount a specific event or incident over and over again (sometimes for years), but they never really let go and move on. In order to let go of a painful experience, the trapped energy related to the experience has to be released.

The Wound is the area in your consciousness that connects painful experiences to cellular memory in your body. For example, a person breaks their wrist ten years ago and the bone is completely healed, but at times this person still perceives pain in the healed wrist. They're not actually experiencing pain on the physical level, meaning that on physical exam there is no swelling or irritation to the nerve endings in the wrist, but the physical cells are *remembering* when they did have pain. An emotional example is when you remember someone who broke your heart or betrayed you many years ago, and it still hurts to think of that person today. This is your emotional cells remembering the pain as if it just happened. Time does not heal all wounds. It doesn't heal any of them. The Wound itself has to be healed by releasing it from its trapped and cycling state.

The Wound is the part in the Shadow that defines itself as *being* hurt. It confuses an isolated experience with actually *being* that experience. In other words if you get a paper cut on your finger, the Wound does not say "I have a paper cut on my finger," instead it says "I am the cut." It takes the experience and *becomes* it. Because of this, the Wound is always suffering. It is the part of you that feels like it is never going to get heard, that the suffering will never end. It feels isolated, lonely and abandoned.

In healing work, the consciousness of the Wound is often referred to as a person's *inner child*. This is because the basic structure of the Wound is often created in childhood or at an immature place of a person's growth, giving the trapped energy the emotional maturity of a child. These Wounds repeat their initial experience over and over again (cycling) in hopes of being discovered so that they can be released and healed.

Each person really does create their own reality, but in "creating your own reality" what most people are doing is re-creating what has happened to them. For example, Jane S. grows up in a household where she is repetitively told that she is stupid by her parent. In reality she has an average to above average IQ, but some part of her became wounded by being told she was stupid in childhood. For Jane S. this Wound shows up in the area of her Energy Field that deals with intelligence.

Every Wound in the Energy Field projects itself outward, like a beacon, in order to get heard. Other people will be drawn to the beacon and re-create the Wound for the person. This is the way the Core Essence helps the Wound to get healed. It is the Core Essence that creates the "beacon" giving the Wound a chance to be heard. The energy clusters in the Wound can only be healed if they are released. They can only be released if they are seen. The Core Essence helps you become aware of your Wound by giving the energy a place where it can re-create itself. The Wounded energy draws attention to itself by re-creating the scenario that caused the original pain. The re-created scenario will not always be identical to the initial event, but it will have a similar theme. The trapped energy usually has to re-create the scenario many times before a person decides to go and look at why they wind up in the same unhappy situations over and over again. This is known as *forming a pattern*. If you look at the patterns in your life, they will take you back to an original Wound that is re-creating an event from somewhere earlier. For example, I have met several people who broke the same bone more than once. The bone that keeps getting injured is trying to get their attention in hopes that they will look into *why* the bone keeps getting broken.

In the example about Jane S. who was told she was "stupid," the Wound will draw people to her that either treat her as if she were stupid or make derogatory comments about her intelligence, even though in actuality she is very intelligent. These unhealthy people will keep coming around until the Wound is healed. People radiate thousands of unconscious messages from the areas in their Energy Field that hold energy clusters. Just take a good look around you, especially your relationships, and you will start to see the same patterns over and over again. This will lead you to all of the trapped energies in your Wound.

When I talk of healing in context to a Wound, it is not about physical healing in the same sense as re-setting a broken bone or stitching up a cut. In this definition, healing is the art of guiding a trapped piece of energy back to the Core Essence where it can be released to resume being part of the overall flow in the Energy Field.

Once a Wound is created, it continues to get larger, causing more of a person's energy to become trapped inside the Wound. This is how a fear turns into a phobia, and how phobias just get worse and worse. For example, a person gets a routine vaccination but their Wound defines the experience as "pain" and labels the energy involved as "hurt," trapping the energy in a cluster. The Wound is constantly alert for any other experiences that are similar to the clusters it already has. In the above example, the Wound will be on alert for anything that resembles an injection. And for every injection this person gets, the Wound will store each event in the same energy cluster causing it to get bigger and bigger. After a while, the person can get panicked at just seeing a hypodermic needle or simply thinking about needles; they don't even have to have the experience of getting an injection to increase their Wound energy.

The Wound level is the place inside of you that gives you a feeling of being trapped, or leaves you with the sense that "it will never end," that nothing will ever change, and there is an accompanying sense of hopelessness. These are just some examples of the emotions that derive from the Wound.

To look at why the Wound level defines certain experiences as "hurt" and not others is an individual journey. Certainly not everyone who has received a shot has developed a phobia about needles. It is at this level of the Shadow, the Wound, in which a lot of answers can be found about why you are here and what your gifts are. To discover who you truly are requires that you look into your Wounded Self. Avoiding it will only make the Wound stronger, allowing less and less of your Core Essence to flow into your consciousness and into your life.

Statements of:

The Belief System

CHAPTER SEVEN

Belief System

The Belief System is filled with all of the individual beliefs a person holds onto. This can be thousands to millions of independent beliefs held in a person's Energy Field. Beliefs are statements that people hold onto as "facts." They take these "facts" and then live their lives as if they are the truth, the whole truth and nothing but the truth! The real Truth is that they are **not** truth but simply beliefs, or statements that the conscious mind accepted as "facts" during some point in life. Remember, just because a person thinks chunky peanut butter is better than smooth peanut butter does not make it a Truth for all. It's just an opinion, a personal "fact" that this person prefers chunky peanut butter to the smooth kind. Not a universal Truth, but rather a personal belief.

When we are born, the majority of our energy is still flowing strongly from the realm of our Higher Self to the reality of present time in our Lower Self. In other words we understand the big picture pretty clearly. But every moment that passes after a person is born they start looking more and more to their Lower Self to define reality, forgetting the Knowing and Truth that comes from their Higher Self. Along with this process, a person starts attaching to the beliefs, experiences and statements of the people and the world around them.

An example of this is a little blonde girl born to two brunette parents. Let's say the parents have a belief that says blonde people are less intelligent than people with brunette hair. All beliefs are held clearly in our Energy Fields. Even if the parents never verbalize that they believe their little blonde girl is less intelligent than brunettes, she'll get the message from their Energy Fields. If the little girl takes on this belief from her parents, she will then distort her IQ accordingly. Not only will she distort her own intelligence, but she will wind up holding a prejudice towards all blondes for being unintelligent and all brunettes for being overly intelligent. The real Truth, of course, is that hair color and intelligence have nothing to do with each other.

A person generally collects the majority of their beliefs in childhood, though we certainly take on plenty as adults. We can also bring beliefs in with us when we're born. As a human being part of why we are here is to explore ourselves, and the Belief System is a great vehicle for doing just that. This is because our lives are products of our beliefs. If a person is unhappy with something in their life, chances are they will try to understand why they're unhappy and then change it. Any time a person starts questioning themselves or their life, it will take them into an exploration process of their Belief System. Through this process of learning what's really Truth versus a false belief, you are eventually led back into your Core Essence.

To explore a specific set of beliefs, a person's spirit may choose to be born into a family that has the same exact beliefs which reinforces them. This gives the person a strong experience about living with people who have the same set of beliefs. Another option is to choose a family that has a complete opposite set of beliefs. This can help a person to challenge their beliefs, exploring them from a more aggressive angle. Either way, a big part of what we are doing here is experiencing our individual and group beliefs. People make decisions to continue on in certain beliefs, going deeper into them, or to let go of certain beliefs altogether. Either decision will result in seeing the world from a different place.

An example of this is religion. Let's say your belief is that Christianity is the best religion out there. As a soul, if you are exploring a belief that says one religion is superior to another, you may choose to be born into a devoutly practicing Christian family in the Middle East, where Christianity is the minority. This is certainly going to challenge you to look at the differences in religious beliefs. On the other hand you may find yourself born into a family that practices Buddhism while you are still functioning from the (unconscious) belief that Christianity is the best religion. This would be another way your soul could choose to explore this particular belief. The bigger reality is that in either example the lifetime is **not** about Christianity but rather the experience of living life with a specific belief from two very different perspectives. From the soul's perspective it will explore every angle of a belief until it can truly define Truth from a limited and distorted belief.

Beliefs are what help us to grow. We would never have gotten out and explored this wonderful planet we live on if we didn't *believe* that there was something else out there. We would never have climbed mountains, sailed the ocean and crossed vast lands with nothing to go on but passion and intuition. We would never have gone to the moon. We would stagnate without beliefs. The ultimate belief is that we are everything and everything is us. This is another way of saying we are God, God is within everything. Beliefs can be very expansive as the above examples show. The beliefs found in the Shadow Self are the negative beliefs that limit us. The beliefs found in the Core Essence are Truths.

If you grow up in a household that is vegetarian and you are raised to believe that this is "the healthiest way," you could be missing out on a lot. How do you know if you like meat if *you* don't try it? What if you have a body that functions better on meat? As the saying goes, you'll never know if you don't try!

Beliefs are learned not only from our family but also our education system, friends, extended family, religious upbringing, television, magazines and the country that you grow up in. For that matter the city and state that you live in have their own beliefs. Inside the United States, just try moving from the East Coast to the West Coast or from the North to the South. It can be like moving to another country! Every geological area has its own unique history and culture. This is what makes up social customs. It's these social customs that often hold the beliefs of an area.

You can live in an area and not get caught up in the beliefs that are held there. This is part of what finding your Core Essence is all about. When you are connected to your Essence, you live by your own Truth, not the beliefs found in a certain area or culture. You stay true to yourself no matter where you are at. You don't conform. You don't rebel either, you just live in your own Truth.

The beliefs that a person chooses to live by are an integral part of their overall attitude towards life. We do create our own reality, so your attitude towards life has a lot to do with the actual life you are living! Your day-to-day life is created from the information that's found in your Energy Field. This is because the Energy Field is the container, or blueprint, for your life and this "container" is filled with your beliefs. Exploring your beliefs will lead you into any distortions that are held in your Energy Field and conversely, if you start by exploring the distortions in your Energy Field, you will be led into your beliefs.

For example, a person has a lot of beliefs about the concept that life is a hard, continuous struggle filled with nothing but trials and suffering—no gain without the proverbial pain. If these are the beliefs in charge, then the person's life will indeed be a struggle. It will be filled with drama and pain. Success will only come if this person has suffered and struggled. No pain, no gain? Okay, says the person's Energy Field, I'll create that for you.

The consciousness of the Belief System is one of the messengers that tell the Energy Field what to do. *The Energy Field is simply the blueprint.* It is changed by whatever is telling it to change. So if you're in your Core Essence, then that's where you're creating your blueprint. If you're in your Shadow Self, then that's what's in control. In order to come from your Core Essence you have to explore and release the negative beliefs held in your Shadow Self. This is where sayings like "showing your true nature" come from. Are you living your life from your True nature or from learned behaviors? The more a person dissolves their Belief System the more they live from their Truth, their Essence.

From this perspective you can see the benefit of becoming well acquainted with your own beliefs. If they serve you, that's fine. However, if your beliefs don't match what you want to create in your life, what you truly desire to be, then you're going to have to find, explore and release the beliefs that aren't working for you. Your outer reality is simply the physical manifestation of your inner reality. You can't change the outside, your health for example, without first changing the inside.

An example of this is a client who comes into a healing session with a complaint that they never have enough money and are always in debt. From a healing perspective, the deeper question is not about how much money they make or what they spend it on, it's about uncovering the beliefs the client has about money. Money issues are rarely about money but usually part of a bigger situation involving certain belief patterns.

Many of my clients have presented to a healing session complaining about their finances. Most of the time the issue was not about the money itself, but rather self-responsibility and the beliefs they held around the concept of being self-responsible. Some had nurturing issues and deep inside they unconsciously stayed in debt with a hope that someone else would come along and get them out. In other words, someone would come and rescue them. Or they didn't want to take responsibility for the choices they had made regarding money, like not shopping around and paying too much for a new car or a house. Another example would be going into debt for a child by sending them to an expensive, private school when the parents could not really afford it, or spending their money on other people with an unconscious hope that they will be popular or well-liked.

In these cases, the healing process is not so much about what the client is or is not doing with their money but *why* they are doing it. What drives their behavior? One of their beliefs is behind the wheel! If the person wants to change their reality, then they need to change their behavior. This will require them to get back in their own driver's seat. You have to identify, and then release the beliefs that are controlling you. This will help you to take conscious responsibility for your life.

It's that last part, "taking conscious responsibility" that often triggers people. On some level we want to be empowered, but on so many other levels most people want to stay helpless victims. To change this you have to examine your beliefs by looking at why you do what you do, and why you believe what you believe. Does it come *from* you or was it taught to you? Identifying and releasing the individual beliefs that make up your Belief System is the process of dissolving this level of your Shadow.

Statements of:

The Defense System

"I am not responsible for anything!"

"If we don't hear it then we don't have to deal with it"

"Stay in your box. You can't handle the world on your own"

"If we can't see it then we don't have to deal with it"

"If we don't acknowledge it then we don't have to deal with it"

"Deny everything"

"NO! Don't think for yourself. I'll take care of everything"

"I will only take credit for the good stuff!"

"If anything scares you I'll make it go away"

"If anything hurts you I'll make it go away OR I'll help you forget it through drugs, alcohol, food, joking...a coma"

"I will keep you from facing reality"

CHAPTER EIGHT

Defense System

The Defense System sits in the middle of the Shadow. It has the job of protecting the Belief System, Wound and Magician while promoting the Idealized Self-Image and Mask. It is very good at what it does.

There are five separate defenses that create this level. They are defined as *Schizoid*, *Oral*, *Masochist*, *Psychopath* and *Rigid*. Each defense pattern defines a person's behavior in terms of their character as well as the motivating factors behind their character. When you're studying someone's character, you are studying their traits, how they portray themselves to others as well as themselves. This deals with looking at a person's overall way of acting. There is often a huge distinction between how someone "acts" and who they really are. In a nutshell, when you're looking at someone's "character," you're looking at a false projection that someone is displaying versus their True Self. The study of someone's personal character is known as Characterology, so the formal title for each defense would be *Schizoid Characterology*, *Oral Characterology* and so on. Characterology study was born in the 1930s when a psychiatrist started to notice consistent behavioral patterns in the way people acted. By the 1960s these same patterns were also noticed by people working with Energy Fields.

Not only does someone's behavior show these five consistent patterns, so does the actual structure of their Energy Field. The Energy Field changes itself into five different patterns depending on which defensive behavior is being displayed. Each of the five patterns creates its own unique shape. When a person is in the *Schizoid Characterology*, their Energy Field looks different than when they are

44

in the *Oral Characterology*. It's the Defense System that has the most input as to what form, or shape, someone's Energy Field takes on.

The consciousness of the Defense System can be thought of as the glue that holds the Shadow Self together. It separates the Belief System and Wound from the Mask and the Idealized Self-Image. It creates a split between these two areas but still keeps the structural integrity of the Shadow in tact. The split keeps a person from being aware of their Victim Consciousness. For example, a person could be going through a separation and be in terrible emotional pain, yet they can still go to work and function as if nothing is wrong. The emotional pain (Wound) and the person's ability to function (Mask) are kept separate by the Defense System. It convinces the consciousness that everything is "okay," in hopes of keeping the consciousness away from the Wound. This is the clever way the Defense System keeps the Wound intact.

So why does the Defense System want to keep conscious awareness away from the Wound? The Defense System works for the Magician. It's the Magician's second-in-command. Remember, the Magician is the part that wants to have power *over* God, not return to the consciousness of God. So it is the Magician that created the Defense System in order to convince the Victim Consciousness (Wound/Belief System) and the False Image (Idealized Self-Image/ Mask) that it is there to protect them, to take care of them and to keep them alive. It is the Magician who plays at being a God that promotes a person to stay small and un-empowered versus the real God who supports a person to grow and evolve into their own personal place of empowerment.

As you've learned, the Wound has its own consciousness which is referred to as the inner child. It is indeed childlike, looking for someone to come along and take care of it. It looks for someone, or something, to make the pain and loneliness go away. This is where the Magician steps in, telling the inner child that the Defense System will protect it and be a loving friend—as long as there is still pain and loneliness to protect! This motivates the Wound to stay in pain so that it doesn't lose its new best friend: the Defense System.

The Belief System consists of all the negative beliefs a person has. It does not want to be healed of those negative beliefs because if the beliefs are released, then the Belief System ceases to exist. The Belief

System encourages the defenses to take over and protect all of the negative beliefs so that it can continue to exist. It too has a strong motive to give its power over to the Defense System.

The Defense System uses the power it gets from the Wound and the Belief System (which is pure energy) to build a strong False Image. The stronger a person is in either their Mask or Idealized Self-Image, the more energy they have routed through their Defense System. In other words, someone who is deeply in denial is deeply in defense. Each individual *Characterology* is used to defend a specific level of the Shadow Self. There are five levels in the Shadow Self (not counting the Defense System as it is the one doing the defending) and five *Characterologies*. So each *Characterology* is partnered with a specific level of the Shadow Self. A marriage built on denial. The marriages are as follows:

The *Schizoid Characterology* works with the **Magician.**

The *Oral Characterology* works with the **Wound.**

The *Rigid Characterology* works with the **Belief System.**

The *Psychopath Characterology* works with the **Idealized Self-Image.**

The *Masochist Characterology* works with the **Mask.**

The Defense System uses the majority of a person's energy. Because of this, more time will be spent explaining each individual *Characterology* and how it functions in a person's life.

Statements of:
The Idealized Self-Image

"I know myself pretty well. I don't think there's much someone else could tell me about myself that would be a shock because I know everything already"

"Well, I've only taken one class, but I could teach you a lot. I pick up things quick like that"

"If you let me, I could really help you"

"Ahuh, hmm ... yeh, I already know that ... hmm, hmm, yeah, I get that too ... no, I got that ... I know that already, hmm ... I know that too ... No, I already understand ... hmm, no, I got that...."

"If you take a closer look, you'll see that I'm clearly not to blame for any of this"

"I'm doing this for your own good"

"If you'll just see this my way..."

"I believe this is your issue, not mine"

"If everyone else would just do what I say, we would be better off"

"You know, the problem's not really with me..."

CHAPTER NINE

Idealized Self-Image

To understand the Idealized Self-Image, it's important to define 'self-image' first. This is because a person's *self*-image comes from the Shadow and is not a true description of who they really are. A person's *True* image is defined from their Core Essence.

A person's self-image is based on their individual beliefs. This makes a person's self-image a mirror of what they *believe* to be true. Not real Truth, but Shadow truth. For example, if a person believes that they need to weigh 110 pounds to be beautiful, then their self-image will be reflective of this. The person will not even feel beautiful at 113 pounds. They will only feel beautiful at 110 pounds. And if you *believe* you are stupid, then you will look in the mirror and see a stupid person looking back, no matter how intelligent you really are. We believe our beliefs, therefore we believe our self-image.

Since all the beliefs in the Shadow are learned statements (from places like schools, parents, television, friends and religion), this means that **the self-image is based on outside influence.** Someone raised in Asia is going to have a different definition of physical beauty compared to someone raised in Canada. And the definition of physical beauty in 1720 England is very different than New York City today. Physical beauty is just one example taken out of the thousands of beliefs a person holds onto. There are beliefs regarding money, education, socialization, ethics, science, religion and so on that affect a person's image of themselves. In one family, being wealthy may be a goal that they teach their children to achieve.

Another family may say money corrupts. It is from these learned beliefs that a person reaches adulthood with a self-imposed definition of who they are and what they should be like in the future. All these beliefs combined create a false self-image. It is only when someone is coming from their Core Essence that they let go of learned beliefs and live their life from what they Know to be true, instead of what they have learned to define as truth.

The self-image is impossible to live up to. How could any one person stay in the boundaries of what their parents, friends, religion, school and mass media are all telling them to be? They can't. No one person could possibly be all those beliefs at the same time. This is especially true because most beliefs are contradictory. Religion tells you to never lie, yet you see your parents lie all the time. They may have a "reason" or call it "a little white lie just so we don't hurt grandma's feelings," but it's still a lie. Mom says "stop whining" but you really have to go to the bathroom and you can't get her attention any other way. How do you stay mommy's perfect little girl yet still get her attention so that you can get your personal need met? The Belief System holds a person in prison, not allowing them to just be who they are. People spend a great deal of their energy and time trying to be something they are not. Your Belief System tells you how you should look, act, think and behave—but it's not the real you. The real you is only found when you let get of your beliefs and come from your Core Essence.

It is the job of the Idealized Self-Image to put a positive spin on the negative Belief System. It will try and make the self-image look good, no matter how unpleasant the belief is that's being expressed. It will use some sort of justification for a person's behavior. This is seen in the above example where the parent lies but then makes it seem pretty by calling it "a little white lie" and justifies it by saying she's lying so she does not hurt grandma. The simple truth is she's not telling the Truth. A lie is a lie, little or big. This does not mean I'm standing in judgment of lies being good or bad. I'm simply stating that a person is either in Truth or they are not.

The Idealized Self-Image is the part of the Shadow that makes being in darkness look good. It's got an excuse and a rationalization for everything. It uses blame, avoidance, justification (commonly seen when someone is throwing out statistics!), sarcasm and projection just to name a few methods. This is why people who smoke like to be around other people who smoke, alcoholics want to hang around with other people who drink, and someone who is expressing prejudice wants to be around other people who have the same prejudiced opinions.

Humor is another common method used to express beliefs that are dark. Television sitcoms do this on a regular basis by using sarcasm and jokes as an illusion to cover up something negative, making it seem like it is acceptable just because people laugh. The Three Stooges hit each other all the time, yet this was supposed to be okay because the violence was defined as humorous. On the old show, *The Honeymooners,* the main character continually threatened to hit his wife if she didn't obey, but because he claimed to love her, this was supposed to be funny. Today's sitcoms have taken this to even more graphic levels which often involve shaming and humiliation. The Core Essence, which radiates only Truth and love, would never threaten violence or humiliate. Despite many popular songs, true love does *not* hurt. Not physically, emotionally or mentally.

The overall theme in the Idealized Self-Image is to "make it look good" no matter how dark it really is. Frequently this is done in the form of superiority. This is the part of the Shadow that believes it is better than other people. Because its job is to make itself look good, it will even try and make superiority look nice and acceptable.

When someone is in their Idealized Self-Image, they do not accept that there is anything negative about themselves. This is how they maintain the illusion that they are superior in some way. For example, someone may point out that a particular friend's issue is anger. The friend will see that they have anger but will quickly justify it. An example of this would be a statement like "I know I'm angry, but it's just because my husband makes me so mad." They justify their anger by projecting the responsibility of *their* anger onto a spouse. This way, the friend does not acknowledge any responsibility for their own anger. The friend is not in denial that they have anger, but they're blaming their anger on someone else, maintaining an illusion about themselves that they don't have any ugly traits because, after all, that ugly anger is not their fault.

It is significant to understand that all emotion comes from within. Another person may trigger, or bring out, a particular emotion, but the emotion itself is still yours. Emotion comes out of a person's hormonal system. Nobody else can possibly be using your hormonal system, so if you're angry, it is *your* emotion. Another person or situation is merely a mirror for the anger that is already inside of you. In a healthy scenario, when a person is angry, it is the responsibility of that person to look within themselves if they want to understand what the anger is really all about. I am not saying you shouldn't express anger, but projecting the reason as to why you are angry onto someone or something else is a way of avoiding your own Shadow Self behaviors. For example, a person can be angry because it is raining outside and they were going to go to the zoo. They may blame the rain for "ruining their day," but if they stop blaming the weather and looked inside themselves instead, in this example they would find a belief that says "I never get to have any fun." They are not really angry at the rain, the rain just triggered an old Wound that reacted by expressing anger. All emotion is triggered by something deep inside a person.

The Idealized Self-Image projects any emotion that may be perceived as negative onto another person, place or object in order to keep you away from acknowledging your own pain and your own negative behavior. Another example of this is when a person trips over something left on the ground, then immediately curses the object and yells at whoever left it there. Their Idealized Self-Image keeps them from acknowledging that *they are responsible for tripping* because they are responsible for their own behavior, this includes watching where you're walking.

This is where the saying "passing the buck" comes from. In the earlier example, the person denied any self-responsibility for looking at their anger by projecting, or passing, the responsibility of *their* anger onto the spouse. In this case, they might walk away saying something like "I'm angry, so I hope my husband takes a good look at himself." Their Idealized Self-Image stays intact, and they get to feel superior over the spouse because in their mind they have no issue, but their spouse does!

The Idealized Self-Image can be one of the hardest things for a person to identify in themselves. A suggestion is to start by acknowledging that there are things about you that are just not going to look nice. And to acknowledge that what you define as "positive" traits may actually be negative traits because some part of your consciousness has bought into your Idealized Self-Image.

I have had clients come to a healing who were in sales. They proudly told stories of how pushy and aggressive they were. Unfortunately, they had been fired from their jobs or had frequent complaints from customers and co-workers. They actually went on to increase their pushy and aggressive behavior believing that they just needed to "work harder." It never occurred to them that it is this very behavior of being pushy and aggressive that is the problem. When a person is functioning from their Idealized Self-Image, they have a hard time believing that any part of their behavior is not actually a positive trait, no matter how aggressive it is. It could take this type of person years to see that what they believe to be their best features are actually their biggest faults *unless they are willing to see their behavior in a different light.*

Be willing to see yourself for who you truly are and you will be well on the way to breaking down your Idealized Self-Image and living from your Core Essence. We all have negative traits, and it's the willingness to admit to them that leads to positive changes.

Statements of:

The Mask

"Nope, no problems here"

"Life is just perrrfect!"

"Don't worry, this too shall pass!"

"I'm sorry, did you say something?"

"If you're just nice to people, people will be nice back to you!"

"Problem? What problem?"

"Okay, people, just turn that frown upside down and you've got a smile!"

"Oh, come on now, you're okay. Just remember, tomorrow is another day"

"I'm sure this is just temporary. Soon it will all go back to normal"

"There, there now. Certainly things can't be that bad!"

"Everything will be fine, just fine"

"Oh, wasn't today just wonderful! Hmm... We had an earthquake today? What earthquake?"

"Everyone's upset? Really, what about? Did I miss something?"

CHAPTER TEN

Mask

The Masked Self sits at the outer layer of the Shadow. This is the most distant place your consciousness can get from your Core Essence. This is the farthest point from Truth you can go. The Masked Self displays this well by being the densest, or most solid, aspect of the Shadow. "Dense" is used in the strictest energetic sense meaning that the molecules here move very slowly creating a thick dark Shadow. The slower molecules move, the darker the energy appears, and the slower we are to "see the light." That's where this saying comes from, more literal than most people know!

When someone is in their Mask, the facial characteristics they display are often false in appearance making them easy to spot. They have a smile that is too bright or forced, a laugh that is a little too loud to be natural. They can be smiling when most of the other people in the room are sad or even crying. The gestures and words that come out of the Mask appear insincere and even crass at times. This is because, when a person functions from their Mask, they are as far removed from real heartfelt sincerity, Truth and emotion as a human being can get. This is why it is called a Mask; it represents a false outer cover devoid of any real essence.

The person who is in their Mask may or may not be aware of it at the time. How often have you heard the saying "fake it 'till you make it" or "I can't even remember what I said there." At times most people can acknowledge that on some level they participate in life but are not really aware of what they're doing or why they're doing it, but when someone has a strong Mask, they can be completely oblivious all of the time.

A person in their Mask only wants to see the good stuff all the time, even if they have to make it up. Embellishment is a common trait at this level. This desire to only see the pretty stuff is what keeps the person oblivious so much of the time, because life is never all pretty. In its naked Truth, life is the good and the bad woven together so you cannot see one without seeing the other if you're going to face reality.

A person functioning from their Mask is not in touch with the real world. This does not necessarily mean they're isolated, just not in touch. They'll go to a party and say "hey, wasn't that a great party?" when in reality it wasn't. If asked, the majority of the other people attending the party will attest to the fact that it was an awful party. Another example is when one person insults another person directly to their face. The one with the strong Mask will be oblivious to the reality that they were just insulted. On the same note, someone with a strong Mask will be unaware that their spouse is unhappy even though that same spouse is crying right in front of them. They'll often walk away saying "I don't know why their crying" without even attempting to comfort or talk with the emotionally upset spouse. Or a friend will come to them very upset with a problem. The person in their Mask may feel the pain their friend is in, but it won't last long. Soon they'll be telling the person it's "all right" or "it will soon be over" reaching for a quick fix without truly being present with the other person's pain. I've often witnessed this with parenting. A child comes home with a distressful situation on the playground, in school or the park. The Mask's standard answer is "this is just a phase and they'll get over it" or "tomorrow will be better." This causes children to start seeking guidance outside of the home because the parent was not honoring their pain, just dismissing it as a "phase."

When a person wants to dismiss something, what's really happening is that they don't want to face the situation and take self-responsibility. They don't want to have to deal with the painful side of life. Well, it's there whether you see it or not. And if you don't deal with it, it deals with you.

"We see what we want to see in this world." This saying was created for the Mask. Ten people can be in a room and have the same exact experience but have ten completely different opinions as to what just happened. The person functioning from their Mask will have the least accurate description of what happened, as the Mask is farthest from the Core Essence, which represents Truth. So, yes we all create our own realities, but if you are creating yours from your Mask, you are creating the reality that is farthest from Truth.

A Masked individual lives in their own world. Their unconscious motto is to ignore anything out of their basic routine, deny anything that can potentially cause them pain or confrontation, and *above all avoid Truth*. This is usually not conscious; most of the time a Masked person will tell you that their life is just great no matter what is really happening. They rarely question anything and generally only seek help after a crisis. They never see the crisis coming. This is frequently the person walking around saying "I don't know how that could have happened."

This is a very superficial place to be, not only in the sense of physical appearance, but also the lack of willingness to go deeper into themselves in search of who they truly are. The Mask is comprised of all the beliefs someone has learned in their life. Added to this are their defenses which basically tell them to just believe their Belief System and avoid their own individual thoughts and conclusions about self, life and God. The Mask works very hard to make sure the person never sees any problems in their life or the lives of the people around them. It doesn't mean they don't have problems, just that they don't see them for what they really are. A person with a strong Mask will see their spouse's alcohol problem as "social drinking" and abusive behavior as "just a little stress." A Masked person often uses obsessive behavior to keep themselves busy and away from reality.

As time is speeding up and the world is becoming more complex, peoples Mask's are becoming stronger. This is seen clearly in the rise of cosmetic surgery (an obvious Mask,) self-help books, gurus and therapists who are there just to remind you how great you are. It's also apparent in the apathy people at large have about improving the lives of everyone on the planet. There isn't a problem with improving their own lives, just not anyone else's. The Mask fears that if you look beyond yourself and see anything ugly in the world around you, it might reflect back your own ugly traits. The Mask would be correct. Everything around us reflects something personal back to us as individuals. An example of this is someone going to marriage counseling who just wants the relationship to get better but doesn't want to acknowledge anything harmful or neglectful they might have done in that relationship. They just want to go forward towards some ideal future without owning responsibility for creating the situation they're in. In this case, they just want the marriage to get better without owning their part of how it got bad to begin with.

When you are aware that you are functioning from your Mask, the goal is to stop and look at what you are avoiding. If you cannot identify your Mask, the goal is to learn the specifics of what your particular Mask looks like. What a Masked person has is a failure to see their issues. The Mask keeps you from questioning and growing in life. It is a void.

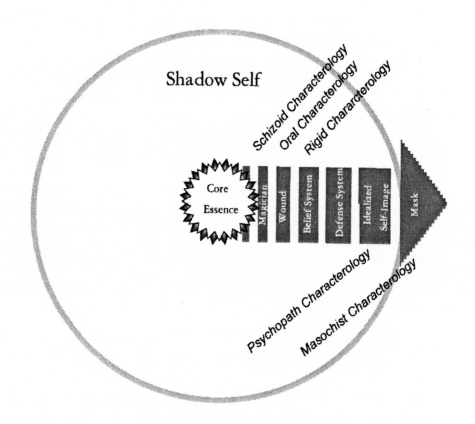

DEFENSE SYSTEM

Each Defense Characterology is paired with an aspect of the Shadow Self. The Defense's job is to make sure the Shadow Self is never destroyed. It does this by strengthening your False Image and cycling you in your Victim Consciousness. The Defense System and the Shadow Self are in a marriage. The marriage is built on denying the existence of your Core Essence and increasing the power of your negative ego.

58

CHAPTER ELEVEN

An Overview of The Defense System

The shape of a person's Energy Field is largely determined by their Defense System. Different defenses distort the Energy Field into different shapes. This is one way the Defense System controls the flow of energy, keeping the Core Essence from moving freely in and out of the conscious mind. If you had a drinking straw and twisted it in some way, the mere act of twisting the straw would distort, or even stop, anything trying to flow through the straw. It's the same principle that the Defense System uses with your Energy Field. It distorts the Field and prevents the energy from flowing in and out of its natural pattern. There are 5 major defenses known as *characterologies*.

The Magician aspect in the Shadow Self tells the Defense System what to do. The basic tools of the Magician are control, manipulation, judgment, blaming, superiority and avoidance. All five of the characterologies in the Defense System use these tools; they just look different for each defense. Some tools are more prominent in certain defenses. Since each characterology defends a specific aspect of the Shadow, if you are familiar with the defenses, they can help guide you into the part of your Shadow that is trying to speak to you right now. For example, the Oral Characterology defends the Wound. One of the personality traits of the Oral Characterology is blaming. So if you find yourself blaming other people a lot, then you know something in your Wound is trying to get your attention.

All five of the characterologies are equal. One is not better or worse than another. They all keep you from your Core Essence. It is the amount of energy you are using in a defense that makes it powerful, not the defense itself. In other words, if you have 70% of your energy in the Masochist Characterology, then that defense is 70% more powerful than the other defenses in that moment. The Masochist Characterology itself is neutral. It is only as powerful as you make it

When people read about characterologies, they often get caught up in judgment. They judge one characterology to be better than another, or one to be more difficult to work with than another. It is not the characterology itself, but rather how much energy someone is putting into a particular characterology that determines how powerful it is. If you are just looking at the specific character traits, the Psychopath is very aggressive and the Schizoid is very passive. It's easy to assume that the Psychopath is "more challenging" than the Schizoid. Not so, the defenses themselves are neutral. Someone who is 40% Psychopathic is less aggressive than someone who is 80% Schizoid. It does not matter that the traits of the Psychopath Characterology are more aggressive than the Schizoid. It's the amount of energy being used, not the defense itself.

It's important to understand that many traits, like acting superior, are present in all five characterologies it just looks different depending on which characterology you're looking at. For example, someone could have the habit of being chronically late. This is a behavior based in manipulation. The Schizoid Characterology is frequently late but the person does not use being tardy to directly manipulate; they do it because they have a poor awareness of time so the manipulation is passive and indirect. The Oral Characterology, however, loves to be late. When the Oral person walks in on a group late, at least for a few moments, they get extra attention. So this characterology directly manipulates in order to increase its negative pattern. Each characterology uses manipulation but in its own way. So understanding how manipulation looks when someone is in the Schizoid Characterology versus the Oral versus the Rigid, etc. is how you can find out what aspect of the Shadow is trying to be heard. In other words, it is not the behavior but rather why a person is doing the behavior that counts. Some behaviors are more prevalent with some defenses, **but it is not about trying to understand behaviors.** It's about letting the behaviors guide you into the unconscious places inside of you that are trying to get your attention.

Everyone wants to be special. The fact is that everyone *is* special, but because most of us are so disconnected from our Core Essence we don't feel special. This is why the Defense System is so powerful. All of the defenses make a person feel special and unique, even if the feeling of being special is from pain. People often play a 'pain game' trying to make their traumas and illnesses seem worse than someone else's. For a lot of people being sick was the only time they got attention. For others it was only when they "won" or achieved something unique. This sets up an adult life where a person doesn't feel special just for being themselves. They only feel special if something dark is happening like an illness, or they are "winning" against someone else, which sets them up for a life of needing to be better than other people.

This also comes in the form of sacrifice. Children often sacrifice their own desires to do what the parent wants so that they can be the "good" little boy or girl. This sets up an adult life of self-sacrifice because the person believes if they just do for others, instead of doing for themselves, they will be special. This is seen frequently in people who want to become healers. They want to "serve" or "sacrifice" themselves for some perceived greater good. Only, God is not asking anyone to sacrifice themselves; He is helping to lead everyone back into their own empowerment, their own God consciousness, not their Victim Consciousness.

Victim Consciousness is what you get when your defenses are in charge. **The Defense System teaches you a false definition of what if feels like to be special.** The more someone wants to feel special, the more power they are giving their Defense System. The more a person can connect to their Core Essence, the more they Know that they are special, therefore they're not seeking to feel special from something outside of themselves. And when you can feel how special you really are, you can see that everyone is special. No one person is more or less special than another. Every life is equally precious.

The most seductive quality of the Defense System is that it *can* make a person feel special, but it is a temporary and false feeling. The defenses do this by making you feel "better than" other people. If you are using any defense, some part of you is feeling (and on some level acting) superior. All the defenses are arrogant; some are just more obvious about it than others.

Look at all the defense characterologies and find the one(s) that you use the most. This will guide you into the darkest places of your Shadow Self. You cannot heal something if you cannot identify it. The defenses are there to keep you from identifying and working with your real issues. If you don't understand your defenses, then you can get caught cycling and cycling in the same old issues. All five defenses keep you cycling. This is the way they keep you from being self-responsible. To the degree that you avoid self-responsibility is the degree to which you keep yourself defended. To stop your cycling you have to stop using your defenses. This requires that you take an honest look at yourself. As you read more about each defense, you will probably recognize some part of yourself in all five characterologies. Look at which characterologies you identify with the most. If one defense doesn't seem more prominent to you than another, you might want to re-read the Psychopath Characterology. This defense works by confusing people, including the person using the defense, so often people do not recognize themselves in it.

Defenses can be a hard thing to acknowledge about yourself, but if you can't see through your own system of denial, you can't find your Higher Self.

Shape of an Energy field that is
not using the Defense System

The Undefended Self

Shape of an Energy field using the Schizoid Characterology

The Energy Field pulls the energy up and out of the body. Some people's Field goes to the right, others to the left. Either way the energy is primarily routed outside the body. This leaves a person very ungrounded, not very aware of their body or the world around them. How much energy a person has outside of the body is directly related to how present they are. In other words, if they only have 5% of their energy in their body, then they are only 5% aware of themselves and what is really going on around them. This is commonly referred to as "spacing out" or "zoning out." Some people live in this state all day long.

CHAPTER TWELVE

Schizoid Characterology

The Schizoid Characterology defends the Magician and is based on survival. Survival requires us to trust in ourselves, so the person in this defense also has strong issues about trust. Most people have issues with trust, but the person who is using the Schizoid defense doesn't trust anybody. They are generally not paranoid, meaning that they don't necessarily walk around believing people are out to get them. They do, however, walk around believing that the world is not a safe place to be.

This defense works by maintaining an open pathway out of the body at all times, like an escape route. It does this by keeping one of the upper chakras open (usually the fifth or the seventh chakra) so that the person can pull their energy out of their body in less than one second if they fear that they are about to get hurt or killed. This is energetic "fight or flight" syndrome!

This was the first characterology created by the Defense System. It was born soon after the Magician was developed. The Magician is the first step in the process of separating from the consciousness of God. This would be similar to a newborn baby getting their umbilical cord cut. It's thrilling because now you're on your own, and it's terrifying because now you're on your own.

When a person is in terror, the instinct to survive is the first thing that kicks in. People don't think when they're in survival mode, they just react. This can take the form of freezing up or running away. The Schizoid defense does both. It freezes the conscious mind and distorts the Energy Field in order to push the energy up towards the head and out the body. This is where the saying "I was so scared I nearly jumped out of my skin" comes from. The energy literally jumps out of the body, leaving the person a shell of who they are. People really do have "out of body" experiences, probably more often than most realize.

When energy leaves the body, it forces the body into functioning with very little resource. An example of this is breathing. The human lung capacity is very large yet few people actually use their lungs completely. It is amazing how well the body functions on a relatively small amount of air. The average number of respirations, or breaths, a person should have in one minute is about 10-12. Most people breathe around 18-22 times a minute. In other words, most people breathe fast and shallow instead of the slow deep breaths the body is made for. Breathing fast keeps fresh oxygen out of the circulation and increases the amount of (toxic) carbon dioxide in the body because it takes slow deep breaths for the lungs to be able to fully intake fresh air and release toxins. People function like this every day, but how well do people really function? Not very well if you look at the amount of illness people develop, including disorders like chronic depression.

This is an example of surviving. People can live with less than optimal oxygen running through their bodies, but how well? If a person is not functioning with their full lung capacity, they are not as alert or as physically fit as they should be. They are tired and not able to digest their food well. Many people complain of fatigue after eating because it takes a lot of work for the body to digest all that food, and the more the body works, the more oxygen it requires.

This is similar to what happens to the Energy Field when someone is using the Schizoid defense. The human body is able to function on less than 1% of the energy that is supposed to be flowing through the Energy Field, but it doesn't function very well. The two primary results of this are decreased physical health (especially the immune system) and minimal *awareness.* This is exactly what the Magician wants, as little awareness as possible so that it is not discovered in its role of impersonating God and it can continue to be the one in control of your conscious mind.

The primary chakra involved in this defense is the first chakra. This is the chakra of safety and survival. If someone is using a strong Schizoid defense, it usually means that there was fear even before they were born. This defense is based on a trauma that has something to do with survival. The Schizoid Characterology is developed somewhere between the time of conception and twelve months old. In human development, a baby's first year is all about survival and learning to trust the world it was born into.

This is the child who was not wanted. The mother may have thought about, or even attempted to get an abortion. This is a baby who was given up for adoption. It does not mean the adoptive parents were not wonderful. They could be terrific, but the child's initial awareness was that they are not wanted.

This is the child who was somehow separated from their parents in their first year of life. The separation could have been a hospital stay. Many children are put into an ICU because of problems at birth, or they develop a severe medical condition in the first year of life and are separated from the parents for a hospital stay. It has only been very recently that parents were allowed to stay with their children in the hospital, and even then they can't stay in most ICUs overnight.

This is the child who suffered some kind of terror or trauma early on. One or both parents could have died. Even in this day and age, many children are sent away to live with relatives in another town or even another country while the parents work, causing feelings of abandonment. The child could have been involved in a severe accident or a fire. They could have suffered physical or sexual abuse. They could have been in a room where someone else was being physically or sexually abused. They could have even been present when someone got murdered or was born into a household filled with violence. They could have been severely neglected, so much so that physical survival became an issue. Thousands of children a year die of Failure to Thrive Syndrome. This is when a child does not have enough care, like basic feeding and diapering, from their parent to the point where they actually die from the lack of care. This is often seen in low income areas where the parent may be on drugs or neglects their child to the degree that they do not care for their child. This is certainly not limited to low income situations.

In any of the above examples, the child can develop a Schizoid defense. The defense is formed out of physical pain or abandonment. Both cause terror in an infant. The first chakra is the chakra most involved with the physical body, so if it perceives pain as an infant, its only defense is to leave. A baby can't verbalize their pain (other than cry which is frequently ignored coming from babies) or physically run away from the pain, so the Energy Field develops a way to escape the abuse. The consciousness leaves.

So where does the energy go when it leaves the body? The energy that is supposed to be inside the body goes out into the Energy Field and keeps going upward towards an energetic realm that is far away from the physical realm. The energy becomes consciously disconnected from the physical body *and* from the Core Essence. This is kind of like a kite floating out in the wind with its string dangling. The kite's not really connected to the wind nor is it connected to the ground. It's just floating around. Now imagine that the person has the kite string tied to their wrist but has forgotten about it. They just walk around the world, doing their day-to-day activities with the kite bobbing along above them. The kite is unprotected because the person is not paying attention to it. The kite can be torn by trees, knocked into buildings and so forth. This concept of sending the energy out of the physical body was a solution created in a moment of panic, but a person does not function well if they live from this place. It leaves the physical body without much conscious energy and the energy that left the body is just floating around. The car is moving down the highway but there's no driver! This can be very dangerous.

Imagine if you saw something that really terrified you. Let's say you walked into your kitchen and stepped on a mouse. You have a fear of mice. It squeals, you scream. You both freeze for a split second before either one reacts. What if you stayed in that split second for years? Not moving, not thinking and not yet able to react or interact with anything around you. What if life went on around you? People just kept going about their lives, coming in and out of the kitchen all the time, but all you do is stand there. This is a little bit what it's like to be in a Schizoid defense. Life goes on around you, but you're detached, not really present. You're not really connected to the physical realm. You're here, but you're not really here.

When a person uses the Schizoid defense, they often say that they *feel* connected. What they don't realize is that they are not connected to the here and now; they are not present, so whatever it is they are "feeling" is not real. They are out of touch, literally, so what they're feeling is not based in this reality. The people around them will attest to this. The person using the Schizoid defense is often described as ungrounded, spacey, not aware, not responsible, not present, cold, detached, unfeeling and not home just to name a few examples. Ironically, they would describe themselves as warm, loving, present and caring. This is because the Schizoid defense keeps most of the conscious energy floating around in a spiritual realm that has a much higher vibration than the physical realm (which is a little bit like being on drugs) and can give a person the false sense of gentle and loving energy. The Schizoid is not in touch with the part of themselves that is holding the kite and living on earth. They identify more with the disconnected spiritual energy than they do with what is happening right in front of them, so they will tell you they feel 'connected,' but people around them easily see that they are not 'connected' to earth.

This means the Schizoid sees spirit as something separate from Man. They believe that you are either floating with spirit or you are in your body, not understanding that their body is made of spiritual energy. This leads to the false belief that, when you are grounded in your body, you cannot be fully connected to God. This is a good/bad or here/there perception which creates a sense of spiritual superiority. When perceptions become narrowed down to an either/or mentality, they are very limiting. **The Schizoid defense does not see that the dark is a part of the light.** That everything is God. Even the Shadow Self evolved from God.

Sometimes when a person has a strong Schizoid defense they believe that their whole body is bad. They really fight the understanding that *only when you are present in your body can you truly be present with God.* The Schizoid defense is the kite flying in the wind; it wants to stay separated from the body and believes that is the only way to be part of God. But our body *is* part of God, because it's the vessel of God. The body is how we walk through this world, so if you want to walk with God, you have to be present in your physical body. Severe hatred of the physical body is commonly seen in children that were physically or sexually abused at a young age.

Since persons in the Schizoid defense are floating around in the spiritual realm and aware of the gentleness and light of spirit, they often believe that they are themselves, very gentle, light and compassionate. Their friends usually have a different opinion. Often when a friend goes to talk about something serious, like a divorce, the person in the Schizoid defense will say something like "everything will be all right" without really connecting to their friend's pain. If you cannot be present with yourself, you cannot be present with someone else. Another example of this is a friend who is looking for support because their child is dying. The person in the Schizoid defense may say something about the child "going to God." They are not present with the horrible pain their friend is going through and they actually cause more pain by being in denial of what is happening in this reality. In this example, the parent doesn't want to hear about their child going to God; all they want is for their child to live. It doesn't matter if there is Truth to what was said; the problem is that the Schizoid person is disconnected from the harsh reality of the parent's pain and the child's suffering. They are not really there for them. Just because a person is physically standing in a room does not mean that they are present with what is going on in that room. When a person is not present with something, they are causing pain; it may be unconscious, but it is still causing pain. The Schizoid person sees themselves as compassionate, but others experience them as being very cold and without heart.

The Schizoid is not very present with any real pain or suffering because they don't fully acknowledge their own physical existence. The irony is that they believe themselves to be so spiritual and compassionate, but because they are not present, they are not connecting any of that compassion and spirit to the earth. This creates a feeling of coldness from the person using a Schizoid defense. In the above example, the parent can become enraged at the lack of real compassion that is coming from their friend. The friend does not feel their own coldness because they don't feel much of anything going on in this reality, so they become confused as to why people get angry at them.

Have you ever taken a car drive that is routine for you, like going to work, and the next thing you know you're just there but you don't really remember too much about the drive? This is similar to what it's like to be Schizoid. You're there but you're not really there. You're not present. Many people float in and out of this state all the time. Once a person has the ability to be Schizoid, they no longer use it just for times of terror. They use it when they are bored and when they don't want to take self-responsibility.

When you're a baby, you don't have the ability to get up and say "no" if you are being abandoned or hurt. As an adult, you do have the ability to say "no," but this is hard to do when your childhood experiences leave you believing that you have don't even exist so you can't possibly have any power in this world. This is what the person using the Schizoid defense feels, that on some level they don't exist. It has only been very recent that any laws regarding children have come into existence. This is because children were not really acknowledged for having any kind of a say on this planet. If a baby's parents don't acknowledge them, and the planet isn't acknowledging them, it's pretty easy to see why they have a hard time acknowledging their own existence.

Once the Schizoid pathway for "escaping" is in place, as adults, many people will use this to avoid taking self-responsibility. For example, someone is in a meeting and they don't really want to participate, so they just zone out, go Schizoid, leaving very little energy in the body in hopes that they won't be seen. If they're not seen, they believe that they don't really have to participate in the meeting. This also takes away their ability to have a voice, or opinion, about what decisions are made during the meeting. Infants and young children are not capable of taking on self-responsibility, but adults *are* and leaving the body is one way to avoid taking responsibility. In this example, after the meeting people are complaining about a poor decision that was made. The Schizoid says "when was that decision made?" as if they were not there. This is their way of avoiding taking any responsibility for participating in making choices. But not participating is a form of participation in itself because you actively give over your power of choice. **The Schizoid defense chooses powerlessness over empowerment** because when they were initially hurt in childhood, the mind actually believed that they were powerless.

On a soul level, no one is powerless. Not even a newborn infant. We create our own lives. This is empowerment in the extreme. If you create your own reality, you have the power to re-create that reality. The problem is that an infant has the mental capacity of an infant, so their mind does not realize that they can re-create events. The deeper understanding is that we set up the traumas in our childhood to live out the dark nature of our Shadow Self. This helps us to find our Shadow Self and experience all that is in it, eventually dissolving the Shadow back into the Core Essence. This explanation is limited if you just use your mind to try and understand it. The comprehension of who you truly are, what life is really about, and the understanding of how God and your soul fit into everything is far beyond what the human brain can interpret on its own. This process requires a strong connection to your Core Essence. God is defined not by what your mind can understand, but by what you Know. Knowing comes from the ability to take in and understand information from all aspects of your Energy Field. Self-discovery is a way to understand who you are and what it's all about for *you*. It is through the process of self-discovery that you find your own place of Knowing.

When a person is in their Schizoid defense they actually have a pretty good idea about the big picture: God, the universe and life. What they don't have is a good understanding about themselves and what's happening in the present. Because this person is not grounded in the present, they have a hard time translating information from the spirit realm into this one. When they are out-of-body, they have a great deal of spiritual knowledge, but the human brain is in this reality, so in order to get the information into the here and now, they have to be able to connect their spiritual self with their physical self.

To be grounded means that you have a point of reference for reality. An example of this is your body. Your body is a reference point for you. It's so natural you probably don't even think about it. You identify with your body, so when you go out in the world and are surrounded by many "bodies," you have an ability to understand that you are a separate form, an individual. Newborn babies don't have this ability. They start learning about it from the moment the umbilical cord is cut. Most infants go through a period around six to eight months old that is labeled "stranger danger" because the baby often screams if anyone other than mommy or daddy holds them. This is because they are just beginning to comprehend that they have their own body, separate from the parent. Until then, they did not have a point of reference for themselves. They still saw themselves as connected to the parent. Like an appendage. They did not understand that they had their own individual body. As soon as we have this concept developed, we can use our body as a reference point. You can identify someone as "you" because you can identify yourself as "I."

Point of reference is a basic principle used in physics. Another example is the sun. It's often used as a point of reference when describing the universe. We say that the earth is the third planet from the sun when describing the earth's location in the universe. Our concept of night and day, even time, is based on the rotations made around the sun. The sun is the reference point, or constant, for any description of the universe.

The person using the Schizoid defense is not that aware of their body so they lose their point of reference for their individuated Self. They believe themselves to be the kite, not the person holding the kite. People who use the Schizoid defense are often drawn into intuitive professions like healing and psychic reading because of their spiritual connection. These people can usually streamline lots of information from the spirit realm. This is known as "channeling," but the problem is most of the information is not accurate because they don't have a strong reference point for their body. In other words, they are just yelling out whatever information they get in the wind. They don't understand what the information is or if it is really Truth. If a person is not grounded in this reality, then it is hard for them to discern what's really True. They can get a lot of information but it doesn't mean that it's accurate.

People tend to be drawn towards someone using the Schizoid defense because you can feel the spiritual energy surrounding their upper chakras. This can be a very seductive defense, but it is not real. You can feel the spiritual energy, but since it's not grounded, that "spiritual energy" can be connected to anything. All spirit is not light. Just like we have people doing dark things on this planet, there are plenty of spiritual energies doing dark things. How do you know that you're really channeling Archangel Michael? Just because the energy told you it was Archangel Michael? If you can't even identify your own body, how can you be sure to whom you're really talking? You have to be able to identify yourself in order to identify other people. You have to Know your own point of reference to have any sense of accuracy.

The only way you can truly discern dark from light is if you are present in your own physical body. To be fully present in your body you have to have all seven chakras open. This will bring your energy into your body naturally. This is the definition of grounding: having your energy *inside* of your body. One of the goals of any spiritual growth is to be able to ground your spirituality into your life. First you have to start by grounding your spirituality into your body. This is how you find your True Self. This requires your spirit and your physical body to be connected as one.

When a person is grounded, they become aware of everything inside of them as well as around them. *This means the good and the bad.* People in the Schizoid defense avoid looking at anything bad because it reminds them of their traumas. But if you only look at the light, the darkness will come up from behind and bite you. Avoidance is never the path to awareness and growth. Face your traumas and your fears. It's the only way they will ever heal.

Shape of an Energy Field using the Oral Characterology

The Energy Field is more rounded down in the pelvic and leg area. This is because the energy gets stuck in this area, not allowing for the second chakra to receive the full amount of nurturing energy that it requires. The second chakra then sends a stream of energy outside of the Energy Field in search of the nurturance it's not getting from within. Obsessive behaviors like eating disorders, drugs, alcohol, repetitive hand washing, smoking, obsessive thoughts about life events and/or other people all come out of this characterology. The Energy Field is looking for care and nurturing outside of itself. This cannot be found, as you can only draw healthy situations and people to you to the degree that you can nurture yourself.

CHAPTER THIRTEEN

Oral Characterology

The Oral characterology defends the Wound and is based on a lack of nurturance. When we are in infancy, especially under the age of two, nurturance is a primary concern. We don't just need food, water and air to survive. We also need physical contact.

Nurturance is being held, touched, and listened to. This is meeting a child's emotional needs, having someone spend time with them and play with them. Being fully present with a child is nurturing at its best. Human nature is very social. It's a part of our make-up. Feeding and clothing a child is meeting the needs of basic survival but it is not necessarily nurturing. Nurturing is the time spent making eye contact, talking with and touching a child. Sitting down with them as they play with their blocks or reading to them. Listening to what *they* have to say. Nurturing is the difference between breast feeding (or bottle feeding) a child while cuddling and talking with them versus holding a bottle from a distance, or doing a task like watching TV or talking on the phone during the feeding. Nurturance is beyond basic interaction. It is when one person is truly present with another, giving them their full attention. A parent can love their child but not be able to nurture them due to their own wounding. Nurturing is usually a learned skill and, if a parent didn't receive it as a child, they often have a hard time nurturing their own children.

Nurturing gives an infant space where they can express themselves, and let their true passion open up. When a small child is coloring, a parent who is nurturing that child encourages them to try all the colors and gives them space to do whatever they want while maintaining healthy boundaries. The child may want to color on the walls, so a parent can explain to them that the walls are not for coloring but then give them options like a coloring book, a coloring board or plain paper to work with. They can even tape coloring paper onto a wall. In this example the child is given a healthy boundary and still allowed to express themselves. Nurturing becomes controlling when the parent tells the child what they can and cannot color. For example, telling them that they have to color the sky blue. This does not leave space for the child to express themselves; instead it forces them to repress themselves and do what the parent wants.

It is not the outward displays of affection that count in life. **It's the underlying motivation that is important.** Mom could have homemade cookies waiting on the counter when the kids get home from school, but if she is not loving and caring when the kids are grabbing for the cookies, she is not nurturing. If she baked the cookies because of appearances, or because that's what her mother taught her to do, it doesn't make it nurturing. She could be expressing unspoken resentment while the kids are eating the cookies because she didn't make the cookies out of unconditional love. She made them because she thought she had to in order to be a "good" mother. Nurturing involves doing things because it is a natural part of your expression, because in your heart you want to do it. If you don't love to bake, don't force yourself to just because you have kids. That's what a bakery is for. If you force yourself to bake for your kids, the only thing your kids will really feel is resentment. This is the opposite of nurturing. Nurturing is giving, resentment is taking.

It is in the nurturing phase of human development that we discover who we are: individual characteristics, likes and dislikes, natural aptitudes and so forth. The chakra involved in this is primarily the second chakra. This is the chakra of passion and emotion. Many people grow to adulthood with a dysfunctional second chakra, which leaves them unable to express their true emotions, *or* they wind up expressing emotions all the time, making life one long drama. Either way they are using the Oral Characterology to re-live something that was not given to them in childhood: care and nurturance.

As an adult, someone who is Oral is very needy. This is not always so obvious. Lots of needy people initially appear giving. They are the friend that is always there for everyone else, donates time and effort to different causes, always a shoulder to cry on. The catch is that they want something in return. They are keeping a silent log of all the things they do with an expectation that someone now owes them. Often it's generic; they believe that God, the universe or both owes them. Everything they do has a string attached to it.

Nurturing is unconditional. If a person doesn't get real nurturing as a child, then a person does not learn how to be unconditional in giving or receiving as an adult.

The job of any defense is to keep the Shadow Self alive and well. Defenses are there to keep you cycling in your Shadow. In this case, the Oral defense keeps a person cycling in their Wound. The premise of the Wound is that you are hurt. The premise of the Oral Characterology is that you are never being nurtured, or getting your emotional needs taken care of, that you are constantly emotionally hurt. This defense keeps a person believing (and often complaining) that they never get what they want in life. The defense will re-create the "neediness" over and over again to maintain the Wound. The Oral defense does not want the Wound to get healed because if the Wound is healed, the defense is out of business.

A basic, but common, example is when a person stays in an unhealthy relationship. They will frequently complain to friends how unhappy they are, yet they always have an excuse as to why they do not leave the relationship. They create their own misery. The Wound says "I never get my emotional needs met." The Oral defense says "I'll make sure you always stay in an unhealthy relationship so that the Wound stays intact."

The Oral defense is fed by emotional misery. The more miserable someone is, the stronger the Oral Characterology becomes. This is how people cycle deeper and deeper into misery and depression. When something happens that a person doesn't like, their options are limited to either taking some time to see why the event happened and own responsibility for creating their part of the event, or they can complain. The first option is gratitude, the second option is blame.

Gratitude comes from taking self-responsibility and being thankful that you have now increased your awareness and will make healthier life choices. In the above example, this person's friends see that they are in an unhealthy relationship, but the person themself does not. If they stop and look at their life, they will learn what a healthy relationship is and discover how they came to be in an unhealthy relationship to begin with. This gives them greater awareness of their True Self and will empower them to make healthier decisions in the future. When a person slips into blame, it stops the whole process of self-discovery and empowerment. The energy just cycles over and over in blaming someone or something else. To blame is to avoid accepting the responsibility that every person has in creating their own reality.

Every time a person is in a state of blame, or lack of gratitude, they are increasing their Oral defense by feeding it the energy of blame or ungratefulness. Being grateful starts the process of dissolving the Oral Characterology by pulling the energy out of the defense and back into the Core Essence.

This is the second most aggressive characterology in the Defense System. Oral people are very blameful, jealous, spiteful and angry. They are often your instant new "best" friend one day and your enemy the next. They are always looking for someone to blame for their life problems. This is because their Wound is really blaming the parent for not holding and nurturing them as a child. Remember, the Wound holds onto past experiences turning them into energy clusters that are caught in time and held out in the Energy Field. The "wounded" energy does not realize the person has grown up and can care for themselves. It is always looking for someone else to take responsibility for the emotional desires and dreams that go unfulfilled. This is the person who is always looking to be in a relationship. They often want to get married to be 'taken care of.' A part of them does not realize that they can take care of themselves. Men are looking for the proverbial "mother figure" and women are looking for the "father figure."

Instantaneous gratification is the other big issue with this characterology. It is in the nurturing phase of childhood that a child is gradually learning that they cannot have everything they want, exactly how and when they want it. Toilet training is a good example of this. A child is transitioning from a time when they could urinate and have a bowel movement at will, to learning how to take responsibility for their body's functioning. Babies start from a place where they have no responsibility for their bodily functions, but as they become older, and able to control their bodily functions, they are asked to hold their urine and bowel movements until they can sit on a toilet stool. They are physically capable of it, but it takes a little time before they are emotionally ready to take on self-responsibility for their bodies. Most children fight this process because they want to maintain the illusion of instantaneous gratification. They want to do (and have) what they want the instant they want it. This is a natural process of growing up. Each year that goes by we are given more responsibility for our Self. How this is handled in childhood affects how a person handles delayed gratification in their adult lives.

When a person has a hard time with delayed gratification, they have a hard time saying "no" to themselves and others. They have poor boundaries. They want continuous pleasure and never want to deal with anything that is not pleasurable. Addictions like alcohol, food, drugs and smoking all come out of this characterology because they give a person instantaneous gratification. This type of instant pleasure is temporary which is why these behaviors are so repetitive. Obsessive behaviors like frequent hand washing or repetitive thoughts about other people or events are also part of this issue. When someone is having obsessive thoughts or behaviors, they are continually feeding themselves energy by the cycling patterns. It's negative energy but the Oral defense doesn't care, it only sees that it is getting attention and believes all attention is nurturing. This is seen in children who will purposefully bait a parent or a teacher just to get attention. The Wound in them does not care that the attention comes from being yelled at or punished, it only perceives that someone is finally nurturing them.

This is also one of the ways adults wind up in abusive relationships. The Oral part of them perceives abusive attention as nurturance, so they will become involved in abusive relationships in order to get attention. Or they will be very demanding of the people around them, basically be abusive to other people, just so they will get abused back. They do not take responsibility for their behavior. Oral people are so focused on what they are not getting that they don't care how demanding, manipulative or controlling their own behavior is. They believe that they have a right to be abusive because their "needs" are not getting met by other people. They are missing the basic premise *that they have to meet their own needs.*

So, the Oral defense has two primary pathways. The first is that it re-lives the emotional neglect of childhood by continually making the adult a victim through methods like abusive or neglectful relationships; not taking full responsibility for their decisions and behaviors; frequently making unhealthy decisions and "giving" to people who do not give back are just a few examples from this first pathway. The second is that the person themself is the aggressor and becomes abusive towards others so that they can be abused in return. The Oral defense takes the returned "abuse" and gives it to the Wound which increases the energy clusters held in the Wound.

As an adult you can take responsibility for understanding that just because you want something doesn't mean it's good for you. A child has poor boundaries. They can't say "no" to themselves. A responsible adult will say "no" to the childlike need for instantaneous gratification. This is what a healthy boundary is all about, taking self-responsibility and saying "no" to unhealthy choices.

The Oral defense is an emotionally childlike state for an adult to be in. It is in the early childhood that a person wants the world to revolve around them and to have everything they want all the time. It is also in early childhood that we do not have the discernment to understand that what we want may not be good for us. If you let a two-year-old do what they want without any boundaries, they really would run through the house with scissors, play with knives and eat only candy. They could do some serious harm to themselves and others.

Children initially only know pleasure. They release when they want, cry and get fed, fuss and get held. In childhood we gradually learn to give ourselves pleasure as we get older. This comes in the form of gratitude. Gratitude is such a natural flowing state that it is often overlooked when studying the emotional evolution of a child. When a child struggles to build a tower out of blocks, and a parent helps them **but does not do it for them**, the child experiences great joy and learns self-confidence when the project is completed. It is at the time of completion that you can see the joy radiating from the child. Part of the joy that is seen is the gratitude the child has for the blocks, the space to build the tower and the parental support. If the parent does not support the process or controls it by taking over or telling the child how they should place the blocks, the child does not have the same amount of joy at the end of the project. And the child does not learn self-confidence.

Gratitude comes from the joy of owning what you create. Since you create your own life, if you take responsibility and own all that you experience, good and bad, your life would overflow in gratitude and joy. This is not always such an easy thing to do as many people have experienced horrible traumas and illness in their life. This is what makes healing a process. A person can only accept full responsibility for their lives to the degree they can be connected to their Core Essence. The Oral Characterology wants to project all responsibility onto other people or events. In order to get past this particular defense a person has to be willing to stop blaming others.

Taking responsibility for your life will bring you into your Wound, allowing you to heal the Wound. This changes "pain" back to its original form: experience. When you are not holding onto pain, your Wound starts to dissolve and you have less energy in the Shadow and more energy flowing from your Core Essence. You stop seeing life as wounding and start living life as a series of experiences instead.

Shape of an Energy Field using the Rigid Characterology

The Energy Field is very straight. This does not allow the energy to flow freely in and out of the chakra system. A person with this Field will be present but only with themselves. They will have a very limited amount of compassion for the people and the world around them. To have compassion, your energy has to be able to flow freely throughout your whole energy system. This means the energy has to flow up/down, right/left and front/back. In this system the energy is forced to go up and down so much that there is limited energy flowing in the other directions. This means limited connection to other people.

CHAPTER FOURTEEN

Rigid Characterology

The Rigid Characterology defends the Belief System and is based on perfectionism. If your existence could be defined as a "house," it is the outside walls of the "house" that are created by this characterology. The defense keeps all the beliefs locked up inside the house separated from Truth. Truth is what's found outside of the house.

This defense perpetuates the Belief System by making your beliefs seem like the "right" beliefs. The defense is not outwardly aggressive. This means that a person in the Rigid Characterology is not running around trying to get other people to agree with their beliefs (that's the Psychopath Characterology), but it is inwardly aggressive because it works by convincing the person that their beliefs are perfect, therefore they don't need to be changed or even examined. If you feel that your beliefs are perfect, it's unlikely you would go on any journey of self-discovery. The person who primarily uses this characterology is least likely to go into therapy or see a healer. Both modalities are about self-discovery, so if you believe that what you are doing is perfect, you won't see a need to look deeper into yourself. This is how the defense keeps you from becoming more aware.

The defense uses a lot of energy to hold the "walls" of the house together so that the light of Truth does not come shining in from the outside. Because of this, people with a strong Rigid Characterology usually have a high metabolism and are often thin without having to work too hard at staying that way. Sayings like "the shining Truth,"

"Let the light in" and "Let the Truth shine through" were made for this defense.

The main chakra used in this defense is the fourth chakra. This is the chakra of unconditional love and soul connection. The defense blocks the heart chakra so that you cannot easily connect to your soul where real Truth is always found. This gives the Belief System the power to take over and tell the mind what to believe in. Even in matters of spirituality. When someone is in a Rigid defense, they will define God and spirit by what their mind tells them to, not their heart. In order to know the *real* definition of anything, a person has to be able to connect to their spirit.

Of all the defenses, this is the only one that directly disconnects a person from their Core Essence by blocking a chakra. The other four characterologies distort the flow of energy going in and out of a chakra, effectively separating a person's consciousness, but they do not actually block the physical connection between the Core Essence and a chakra.

The person using the Rigid defense has a hard time feeling unconditional love for themselves or other people. They also struggle when asked to feel their own spiritual connection. The heart chakra is the connecting point for unconditional love and spirit, so if it's blocked, it's hard to feel either of these. There are many sayings (in many cultures) about "heart and soul" because these are indeed directly connected. The fourth chakra is the first place in a person's energy system that has this direct connection to the soul level. If you can't feel your heart, then all you're left with are the beliefs you have in your mind.

Rigid people are very intellectual. They rely almost completely on what their mind tells them. In a healing session, they tend to ask a lot of questions about God and spirit. They are always seeking answers from books or other people. This is because they cannot get their own answers from their heart.

They are very attached to their beliefs but they do not realize that beliefs are not Truth, they're merely something that was taught to them or learned from outside of themselves at one time in their life. The other problem is that beliefs categorize and label everything.

That's how you get a belief: you come to a conclusion. So these people want to understand everything but from the very limited place where they categorize everything into a quick answer. They also tend to label and categorize everyone they meet. God is expansive, beliefs are conclusive.

The human brain is merely a holding station. On its own, it's neutral. The brain is filled with trillions of nerve pathways, like highways. The brain's job is simply to maintain the highways. What travels up and down the highways is unique to what each person puts in their brain. This is a form of self-responsibility, for if you are what you think, then you think what you are. In other words, the only thing you "think" is what *you* put in your brain! The brain itself is simply an empty vessel. It does what it's told and then turns around and tells you what to think and do.

If you fill your brain up with your Belief System (which is limited negative beliefs), then what you have is a mind filled with limited and labeled conclusions. If you connect to your heart before going to the brain, you have unlimited, unconditionally loving *experiences* (not conclusions) and a real Knowing of who you are. Most people define themselves by what they're told, not by who they Know themselves to be. The challenge is to fill up your mind with what you Know, not what you're told. Knowing comes from spirit, so you have to be able to connect to your spirit to Know your own Truth.

If your mind is filled with beliefs, it is closed, literally; if it is filled with love and spirit, it is open. How many times in your life have you heard, or even said "try being a little more open-minded." This is a very literal statement in terms of energy. The Belief System is limited. Spirit is infinite in its open, flowing love. The Rigid defense keeps a person living from a closed heart and limited beliefs.

People who are in a Rigid defense are very concerned about being *perfect*. This defense encourages you to believe that your beliefs are perfect, which would imply that you are perfect, to prevent you from exploring yourself. Self-exploration threatens the existence of the Shadow Self.

Perfectionism is the driving force behind this characterology. The problem with the need to be perfect is that it is based on the concept that you *can* be perfect. **Man is perfect in his imperfection.**

There is no possible way anything can be perfect because there is no such thing as perfect. There are opinions, options and experiences, but if you believe something is perfect, then you are limiting what that something really is. The very word 'perfect' is a perception; no two people would define something as being perfect the exact same way. Perfectionism is buying into a belief that says there is a conclusion, or finality. If something is perfect, then it is complete, ended and done, according to this defense.

Life is infinite. We're never "done" and nothing is ever ended. We are constantly changing and re-inventing ourselves over and over again. There are times when we are temporarily complete in something, like the end of one day, but the days of the year are not over. And when the "days" of one year are over, there will be "days" to a new year. Each day by itself is complete, but the days never end. So anything can be complete *for the moment*, but nothing is ever done. So if you say something is perfect, you are implying that it is concluded or at an end. But everything is eternal.

When a person states that something is perfect, they are often making a judgment. The Rigid defense is very judgmental. It judges everything a person does against their Belief System and then concludes whether it is good enough. Because this defense is based on perfectionism, even if a person performs a task that is right out of their beliefs, it could be judged 'not good enough' because the defense is always striving for more and more perfection. For example, if a person believed that they should be jogging two miles a day because they read in a magazine that people who jog two miles a day are better achievers at work, they will train and train until they can easily jog two miles a day. Then the defense says if two miles is good, then three miles is better. Of course when you get to three miles the defense wants you to jog four miles a day. This defense is never satisfied and is always striving for some unattainable goal. It is unattainable because perfection is a perception not a reality, which makes it unattainable.

By the time these people do go into therapy or see a healer they are often devastated by some life event. They are devastated because they believed that if they did everything perfect (according to their Belief System) that life would be perfect. And then something bad happens to them and their (limited) mind cannot understand why it happened because after all, they did everything perfect. In the above example, it is difficult for the Rigid person to understand that jogging and achievement at work don't really have anything to do with one another. Maybe the people who achieved more at work after jogging according to the magazine article they read, did it because they enjoyed jogging and the pleasure from the jogging spilled over to their work. Since the Rigid defense cuts off the heart, limiting the amount of joy they can have, they're not jogging for the pleasure of jogging, they're jogging because they want to achieve more at work. So now they are jogging four miles a day and get fired from their job. They are devastated and fixate on the fact that they were "doing everything right" because they were jogging four miles a day. Their Rigidity in holding onto the belief that jogging increases achievement at work makes it challenging for them to let go and see the situation from a different perspective. I have seen people spend years of their life in therapy doing nothing more than cycling in their Rigid beliefs. The real work is in opening the heart chakra and connecting to spirit so the mind can be filled with something other than learned beliefs. It is hard to let go of your beliefs if there is nothing else to fill the brain. Connecting to the heart is the first step in the process of releasing the need to be perfect. Perfection is an illusion.

When a person is in their Rigid defense they often feel like life will "never end," and it won't. Not in your spiritual form. If your heart chakra is not opened, life becomes drudgery. There is no joy, especially not in everyday tasks. Life becomes something to get through, instead of a series of experiences to be enjoyed or learned from.

Energy is in constant motion; one second is never like another. Life is a series of experiences and it is always changing. It is this very principle that allows you to re-create your life every day. So if you don't like your life today, you can change it tomorrow. This is one purpose of spiritual growth, to be able to connect to the Core Essence and create your life from a place of full awareness instead of living life from a reactionary place. When a person can do this, they are called a Master because they have mastered their Shadow Self and now live from their Core Essence.

In order to change something, first you have to want to change it, and then you have to acknowledge that you have the power to change it. The Rigid characterology stops this process of empowerment (creating your own life) by disconnecting you from your spirit, giving the negative ego an opportunity to come in and tell the person what they should or should not believe in. Because this defense is working on the premise that your Belief System is perfect, it creates a superior feeling in the person who is in the Rigid Characterology. It also fools you that you don't need to change; people around you do, but not you. Your beliefs are fine because they are perfect!

Energetically, this is a very contained defense. It works strictly on the person caught up in the defense. It doesn't waste a lot of energy going outward to anyone, or anything else. And what's really confusing for the Rigid person is that the defense is not really saying that *they* are perfect, just their beliefs. The pain that a person is in when they use this defense is twofold. The first level of pain is because they are cut off from their own heart. The second is because the Wound in their Shadow is feeling its shame, hurt and pain, yet the person's brain is getting the message that they are perfect. This defense does not allow them to express their Wound. They don't *feel* perfect, yet their brain is telling them they are perfect. This strong inconsistency leaves them feeling very isolated and unable to express emotions. If they did express their emotions, they would see that things are not so perfect. People who have a strong Rigid defense usually have a distortion in their second chakra as well as the block in their fourth chakra. This is because the second chakra is the area that deals with emotional issues and emotional outbursts do not fit in with a "perfect" person according to this defense.

Rigid people tend to be very judgmental of everyone around them, yet they often don't see themselves as being judgmental. This is because judgment is so second-nature for the Rigid person that it becomes a natural part of their thought process. When someone is not in a Rigid defense, they are usually aware (on some level) when they are being judgmental. If they don't see their judgment and it is pointed out to them, they will often acknowledge it. To a Rigid person, judgment is the norm. They're basically always in judgment. When their judgment is pointed out to them, they have a hard time seeing what is wrong with being judgmental and will often want to go around and around in discussing the issue. Remember, they use their brain a lot, so when they are trying to figure something out, they will go to their mind versus *feeling* inside themselves for answers. This defense believes that being judgmental is the way to perfectionism. After all, if you don't judge yourself, how can you grow?

Easily, you can grow in love. Growing is not about judging yourself and striving to be better. *Growth comes from unconditionally accepting where you are at right now, imperfections and all.* This includes accepting each and every experience that got you here, even the bad experiences, and loving yourself for everything you have been through. Real growth only comes out of self-acceptance. Real self-acceptance only comes out of unconditional self-love. The rest is merely cycling. When you are striving for perfectionism, you are cycling in your Rigid defense. This keeps you from examining your Belief System. If you don't examine your beliefs, you can't change those beliefs and live from your Core Essence. Like all the other defenses, the Rigid Characterology keeps your energy busy cycling so that you stay in your Shadow.

There is no such thing as perfect. There just is. "Is" has no judgment attached to it. Being in the moment just "is." Letting go of a need to be perfect, or to have the world around you be perfect frees up your energy to deal with what is. This is what being in the moment is all about. Perfectionism is a way of avoiding slowing down and being present in the moment so that you can accept the reality of yourself and everything around just as it is now. If you are always striving for something, then you are not accepting yourself for who and what you are in this moment. If you cannot be fully present in this moment, you cannot be fully present to create the next moment. Perfectionism is like chasing the proverbial "pipe dream." It wastes energy in judgment to avoid discovering that the Belief System is not so perfect. "Let go and let God" is an old saying that reminds us our true path is only found with God. Not with the negative beliefs held in your Shadow Self.

Shape of an Energy Field using the Psychopath Characterology

The Energy Field projects the energy upward, then outside the field in a directed pattern towards a specific person or group of people. There is an underlying purpose to the energy leaving the Field. It is trying to grab the Energy Field of the person (or group) in order to convince them of something. An example of this is a sales person who is trying to get a client to believe their product is the best, or an evangelist who is trying to convince a crowd that their definition of God is the only true definition. This defense is aggressive and *always* trying to get something from someone.

CHAPTER FIFTEEN

Psychopath Characterology

The Psychopath characterology defends the Idealized Self-Image and is based on being "right" and "winning" all the time. Remember, the Idealized Self-Image is the energy that has to make the negative beliefs look good. This defense works by making sure the person using the defense never realizes that their negative beliefs are not such a good thing. Primarily it does this by convincing you that your way is the right way and everyone else's way is wrong.

Seduction is the main pathway this defense takes. Seduction is not always about sex. When you are seducing someone, you are trying to get that person to agree with you and do, say or believe whatever you want them to. Seduction is the act of tempting a person to give in to your way of thinking. Commercial advertisement does this all the time by showing positive outcomes that they imply will only happen if you buy or use their product. Seduction can come in many forms like feeding a person's ego by falsely telling them how great they are or how great they look. It can come in the form of bribery, promises or embellishment. Embellishment is commonly used as a sales technique. The sales person will make their product sound like it is an answer to world hunger, even if they're selling tooth brushes!

Seduction is merely an energy that makes the person on the receiving end feel good about themselves as long as they are in agreement with the seducer. It is when they stop being in agreement that the seductive energy turns aggressive. **This is the most aggressive**

defense pattern in the Shadow Self because it is protecting a person's False Image. If a person's False Image is penetrated they will become aware that their life is not based in Truth. This will lead to discovering their Core Essence and dissolving the Shadow. It is the job of the Psychopath Characterology to stop this process.

The Psychopath is focused on making sure that they are always right. The Rigid Characterology says a person's beliefs are the "right ones" but this defense says the person themselves is always right. If they are always right, then they don't have to acknowledge any of their character flaws. This keeps their False Image intact. In other words, it's their way or not at all. And if you ask them, they'll have no problem telling you why their way is the best!

When one person is seducing another, they are enticing the person to agree with whatever they are telling them. Often this is used in an attempt to get the person to change their opinion or belief about something. Two professions that embrace this characterology are sales and politics. Sales people are hired to seduce people into believing one product is better than another and politicians blatantly say "believe in me." Both occupations spend a lot of time and energy convincing people that *their* way is the best or "right" way.

When someone has to be right all the time, they are approaching life as if it were some kind of battle that they must win. The only way you can really be right all the time is if everyone else is always wrong. This basically creates an environment where the Psychopath is pitted against everyone else. Life becomes a game that they believe they always have to win. If they "win," then they are "right."

Psychopath's can be very talkative when they are trying to get someone to agree with them. They will go round and round in a conversation, going off in many avenues and many non-related examples to confuse the person they are in the process of seducing. Eventually the person on the receiving end loses track of the initial point of the conversation and frequently gives up, gives in, and winds up agreeing with the person. This is a common technique the Psychopath uses to "win" the conversation. They basically wear down their "opponent."

Every day-to-day activity becomes a battle for this defense. It must "win" and be "right" at all cost. This is the person that gets in their car and goes to war against everyone else on the road. Every time they are cut off they take it personally and feel that they have to "get" the other driver. Every other car on the road becomes the "enemy." A simple drive to the grocery store is filled with competition.

These people turn themselves "on" in social settings where they can go and get lots of people to agree with them about any and everything, but then they go home and crash. They use so much energy being "on" that they burn out. They are usually easy to spot because they initially come across very focused, making you feel like the world revolves around you. But as soon as they get what they want from you, they move on. A person using an Oral defense is often attracted to a person using the Psychopath defense. This is because the Oral person is looking for attention. The Psychopath person is looking to use people to their own advantage, so they give complete focus and attention to the Oral person just until they get what they want. Then they leave. This re-creates the Wound of emotional abandonment for the Oral person and makes an easy conquest, or win for the person in the Psychopath defense.

The person using the Psychopath defense is very focused when they want something. They are like the proverbial 'dog with a bone.' In other words they don't let go until they get what they want. The Psychopath defense remembers every time and every person who did not agree with them. They keep a silent log of these events and whenever the opportunity arises, they try and get the person to agree with them even if the initial disagreement happened years ago. This is the person that will bring past events into a present argument. "Don't you remember when you...," they are still trying to get the person to acknowledge that they were wrong so the Psychopath defense can be right. Sometimes they bring up memories from ten or twenty years earlier. They never forget the times that they were perceived wrong and are always trying to get people to change their minds and make them right no matter how much time has passed.

If they can't get a person to agree with them, the Psychopath will go to their friends (sometimes even strangers) and relate the story to them so that their friends can tell them that they were right and the other person was wrong. I once taught a class where one of the students was upset that a friend had not returned a call. On a break, she managed to approach fourteen people and relate the story to them. She made the friend seem "bad" and by the time she was done (under fifteen minutes) she had fourteen strangers agree with her that the friend was wrong to have not called. Another way to look at this is that the student was told fourteen times that she was "right" in less than fifteen minutes. This is a classic thing for the Psychopath defense to do. (So the next time you are quick to agree with someone by making them right in a situation that did not involve you, remember that you just made someone else wrong and you might not even know the person you just passed judgment on.)

The Psychopath defense can go from seducer to attacker in less than a second. If you are not agreeing with them (despite their attempts to charm you), they will become instantaneously aggressive. Underneath their seductive charm is a person that believes life is war that they must win at all cost. If they can't win by diplomacy, then they will win by aggression. They don't give up when they want something and they cross boundaries all the time. This is the person that will hug and touch without permission. They are trying to use physical contact to manipulate. Or they will use repetition to try and wear down whomever they perceive as the opponent.

I had a client once who left eleven phone messages in two hours, all before seven in the morning. There was no crisis, all she wanted was a routine appointment but she wanted to make the appointment right then. She saw nothing wrong with repetitively calling someone just to get what she wanted. The Psychopath defense protects the Idealized Self-Image, making a person believe that everything they do is great. No matter how ugly the behavior, it is this defense's job to make it look good. Another client applied for a job and was told she would be contacted within a week by the prospective employer. When the person did not contact her, this client showed up at the person's office every day and then started following the prospective employer. The client said that she did these things just to give the prospective employer a little more information about herself and answer any questions she might have had. The reality was that the client really wanted the job and was trying to force it to happen but she did not see it that way. She thought she was being "helpful." She was eventually accused of stalking by the prospective employer. The client could not understand what she did wrong, because in her mind she saw herself as accommodating and helpful. She really believed she had every right to do what she did. The Psychopath defense makes every behavior look good to the person in the defense, no matter how aggressive or ugly the behavior really is. The Psychopath will always have a list of what they believe to be rational excuses as to why their destructive behavior is okay. It's the defense's job to make sure this list is very long.

This characterology is where the behavior of stalking comes from. I have met several people who were accused of stalking (sometimes even formally charged) yet they did not see anything wrong with their behavior, no matter how extreme it was. Where the Masochist is in complete denial of all that they do, the Psychopath sees their behavior but never sees it as being bad. It sees everything as Idealized. And it needs to be right so the Psychopath frequently crosses boundaries, i.e., stalking and repetition to get a person to agree with them or give them what they want. Seducing, charming, stalking and badgering are the tools of the trade for the Psychopath defense.

Since life is perceived as a battleground, this defense is very competitive. They are competitive with themselves and other people. This is the parent who pushes their kids in sports and easily becomes aggressive if their child (or the child's team) is not winning. This is the parent who pushes their child into acting, modeling or music lessons. The parent will always tell you that the child 'wanted' to do these things but, in reality, the child did not. Or the child liked to do it for a little while, maybe for a hobby, but the parent's Idealized Image sees a protégé where there is none and pushes the child into something the parent wants, not the child. The Psychopath defense does not allow the parent to see the reality of how inappropriate their behavior is.

This defense is formed when a child is about 4-7 years old. It is the result of parental betrayal. The betrayal is done by the opposite sex parent. The father will seduce and betray the daughter and the mother will seduce and betray the son. The betrayal is often done in the form of promises. If you do this for me, I will do that for you. If you pick up the toy, I will give you a treat. If you stop acting out, I will get you some french fries. The problem is that the parent does not follow through with their promises. This leaves the child feeling very betrayed. They want to trust the parent because what the parent is offering is so seductive; affection, candy, a trip to Playland, attention or love. But they learn to lose trust because the promised treat is not given to them or it is changed. The trip to Playland becomes an afternoon at Grandma's. Even if the child likes Grandma's, it's not the bribe that was originally on the table. The parent plays a game of Bait & Switch or Bait & Deny. They'll either change the original reward that had been promised or deny ever having promised anything, often directly telling the child "I never promised that." This leaves the child confused, doubting their own perceptions and feeling betrayed.

Because so much of the seduction is non-verbal, the child does not really have a clear understanding of what is going on. The seductive promises are often implied, not directly spoken. This is frequently done in the form of affection; an unspoken promise that, if you do what the parent wants, you will get attention and love.

This sets up the premise that life is a battleground. The child learns that if they don't get it for themselves, they'll never get it. This is why they are so competitive. They learn to believe that all promises are false and that it's okay to manipulate. Because they were frequently promised things that they did not get as a child, they model their own behavior after this and make many promises as an adult that they do not follow through on. This is the adult who says "I love you" in the moment, but they don't really mean it. They are just trying to get something from someone. Words and affection do not have a lot of in-depth meaning for the Psychopath; they just use both to get what they want.

Sometimes the parent really does use sexual seduction on their child. This does not mean that they necessarily have sex with their child, but rather that they use seduction in a sexual way to get the child to do what they want. An example of this would be a mother who holds her son and tells him he's her "man" and wouldn't her "man" do anything for her? Then she asks him to go get the laundry. The same scenario becomes even darker when what the mother is looking for is adult affection, and she wants her child to be the one to give it to her. In this case, she doesn't want her son to do a chore, but she wants him to give her nurturance, attention or affection. She wants him to sit down next to her, maybe watch TV with her (it will be an adult program and not a children's program as the parent is doing this to get her need met, not her child's.) She wants her son to hug her and tell her he loves her. The parent is displacing her need for adult affection, and sometimes sex, onto her child.

This child is now being asked to take on an adult role in the house. Specifically, they're being asked to play the emotional role of an adult. On an energetic level, the mother treats the son like a husband, and the father treats the daughter like a wife. This can even take the form of conversation. This is when a mother tells her five-year-old son all about her marital problems or a father comes home and tells his six-year-old daughter all about his work day. I have met women who were either being physically or verbally abused by their spouse and will talk proudly about how their (young) son "saved them." Then they praise the child, believing that this is a good thing. The parent does not realize that she transferred adult responsibilities on a small child. In these examples, the parents are using the children to get their needs met. They want a child to give them adult attention and nurturance. *It is the role of the child to receive nurturance, not give it.*

Remember, it is not the actions of a person that matter as much as the underlying energy. So if a parent is hugging a child because the child wanted the hug or the parent is giving the child affection through the hug, this is healthy. If the parent is hugging the child in order to take affection from the child, this is manipulation and seduction. And if the parent is using sexual energy when they are manipulating their child, the child grows up with a dark understanding of what sex is all about. This is the adult that is a little too close to their opposite sex parent. They are forty years old and still want to please their parent in a way that gives them pleasure in return. This does not necessarily mean that they have sexual thoughts about their parent, but what they do have is a strong desire to please the parent in hopes that the parent will give them attention and affection in return. This is the pattern that was set-up in childhood. Because the child never got the affection that was promised to them (as the parent took affection from the child instead of giving), they are still seeking it as an adult.

The Psychopath defense does use a lot of sexual energy. These people often have very active sex lives. Since they so frequently use their own energy for seduction, they have a lot of seductive energy flowing in their Energy Field so they use it! If they're not using the energy for sex or seduction, then they use it for power. These people often have power-orientated jobs or acting/lecturing/sales careers where they can perform. When someone is performing, they are often seducing a crowd.

This defense characterology uses the third and the fifth chakra. The third chakra being the personality and the fifth chakra is the area of expression. The third chakra is the one initially wounded by the betrayal but it is the fifth chakra most used by this defense. The defense pulls energy up to the fifth chakra, then aggressively sends the energy out to the person/group that it's trying to seduce. The energy is very forceful and will grab the Energy Field of the recipient(s) in order to try and control them. It's similar to one person grabbing the front shirt of another, pulling them forward to hold them while they yell directly in their face. Energetically what the person on the receiving end feels depends on how much awareness they have. Most people feel the pull of the Psychopath, but then quickly become confused and wind up giving in to whatever it is the person wants. This is because when the energy of the Psychopath defense gets in their Energy Field, it goes directly to the brain and causes confusion.

On top of this, the Psychopath is verbally badgering or seducing the other person with lots of words. The Psychopath can get very wordy. Every word they speak gives them an opportunity to send energy cords out their fifth chakra into the Energy Field of the person they are talking to. If the words don't convince you of whatever it is they want you to agree with, the energetic cords that just went in your brain should do the trick.

This is not a pretty defense. But being seduced and betrayed as a child is not a very pretty thing to happen. Everyone has this defense in them, and at some time or another most everyone uses it to get what they want. Of all the defenses, this is usually the one that people recognize in themselves the least. Schizoid people acknowledge that they are fear based, Oral people acknowledge that they are needy, Rigid people acknowledge their perfectionism and Masochists acknowledge that they just want to please others. People using the Psychopath defense rarely acknowledge that they use people, and if they do acknowledge it, they really believe that they have good reasons to be manipulative and will be more than happy to tell you all about it.

In order to dissolve a defense pattern you have to be able to identify it within yourself. This is the first step. The person with the Psychopath defense has to work on their issues of betrayal and the need to win at all costs. One of the challenges that these people face is to be okay with being wrong and losing. Life is not a game. A game implies that what you do does not have permanent meaning and that nothing really matters, because after all this is "just a game." Not true. Everything matters and everything is very real on some level. Life is a series of experiences, but if you are always working to win, then you are missing the experience found in the process of just living. The old saying is true: it is not what's at the end of the road that counts, but rather the journey. If you're fixated on an outcome, you can't be present with the journey. A person using the Psychopath defense could use some grounding so that they can let go of the outcome and be present in the moment to experience their journey. This will bring them into their True Self.

Shape of an Energy Field using the
Masochist Characterology

The Energy Field is heavy, overly round and self-contained. The energy is cycling within the Field, not able to flow freely in and out. This causes a person to be disconnected from present reality. They may take a long time telling a story or responding to a question because the energy in the Field is so stagnate. They also have a hard time forming their own opinions and making their own decisions. They are easily swayed by outside opinions and beliefs, often letting other people tell them what to do.

CHAPTER SIXTEEN

Masochist Characterology

The Masochist Characterology defends the Mask and is based on denying the individual personality. This defense works by making a person blend in, becoming one with the crowd to avoid having their individual perspective seen or heard. It promotes expressing what the group mentality is saying and repressing what the person's own opinion is. The Masochist is the person who has a poor understanding of who they really are in the world and what they want to do with their life. The Mask is the deepest level of denial in the Shadow Self and it is the job of the Masochist Characterology to keep that denial in place.

No two people on this planet are alike. No other person has your exact DNA or your fingerprint. You are a unique individual with your own quirky and wonderful way of seeing the world. You have your own individual opinions, beliefs and your own way of living your life. In other words, you have your own unique personality.

This is the very thing that separates Energy Healing from Western medicine because there are no Standing Operating Procedures (SOP's) in Energy Healing. Energy Healing honors the fact that there are no two people alike in the world. You could have ten people the same age/sex/height/weight present with the same medical diagnosis. All were diagnosed at approximately the same age and have had the same general course in their disease process, yet a healer will work with all ten people differently. This is because *healing works on the root cause, not the disease* and no two people get sick for the same reason. There are certainly some overall generic reasons why people get a specific disease, but if you go beyond the generic understanding there will be a unique reason why each individual person becomes ill.

For example, in Energy Healing allergies originate from the first chakra. This is the generic diagnosis. If you have two clients who are allergic to strawberries, you are going to have two different healings based on the individual reasons *behind* each person's allergy. Knowing that it has something to do with the first chakra is just a start in the overall healing process. Generic diagnoses can be a way to begin a healing, but everyone's disease process, and life issues, are specific to them no matter how generic they may appear on the outside. This is because we are all unique individuals.

From the moment we're born we begin the process of separating from our parents. Especially mom, as she was the one who kept you alive for nine months in her womb. To separate means to individualize. By the time the average child is a year old they are either already walking or starting to walk. Most have mastered crawling. When a child becomes mobile, it begins the process of being able to make a choice for itself and then follow through on that choice. Before they could crawl or walk, if they wanted a specific toy, they would have to count on someone else to get it. Once they can move around, they have the power to make their own desires come true. They can have a thought, make a decision based on that thought, and then move around to make it a reality. They think of a specific toy, they see that toy, and they go get the toy. This is the power of creation! You believe it, you think it, and you do it.

This is also known as autonomy. Autonomy is the ability to do something for yourself. In order to have autonomy you must first have your **own** thought. Then you have to have a desire, or passion, to make that thought a reality. In order to be your True Self you have to start by opening up to your own thoughts. You have to be an individual. We are all born with our own original thoughts, but it is during the time we are becoming autonomous that this process of expressing the True Self can become distorted. To be autonomous, you first have to become individuated.

There is a big difference between a parent telling a small child exactly what to do and giving them the space to figure it out on their own. When we are given a space to figure it out on our own, many individual decisions are made along the way creating autonomy in the mind and body. For example, a parent can tell their child to go clean their room. This is a general statement with a general boundary. They may even make the boundary more specific by saying something like "get your room cleaned up today," but if the parent were to go into the room and tell the child exactly how they should clean the room, where they should put things and what they can or cannot leave out, this becomes controlling. A basic task is no longer autonomous. The child becomes like a robot, not allowed to think for themselves. Instead, they are supposed to do exactly what the parent says. Autonomy has been taken away and replaced with control.

Human nature is based in the flow of creativity. The other name for God is *Creator*. We are an aspect of God, therefore we are creators by nature. As blood is always being pushed out of the heart to feed the rest of the body and keep it alive, so is creative life force being propelled throughout the body with every breath we take. It is our natural state to flow with creativity, and as everyone is unique, everyone's creative energy is unique to them. Autonomy is the ability to express this creative energy.

Many people lose their autonomy before they are even three years old. Loss of autonomy happens when the parent and/or the environment is too controlling. Children need space to grow. Literally, the Energy Field slowly expands as a child grows older, and part of the expansion is the energy moving in and out of the Chakra System. Ideally, the energy is free flowing, allowing for the creative forces to create! It's the job of the third chakra to take creative energy (which originates in the second chakra) and channel it into specific tasks. These tasks include formulating opinions and beliefs. The third chakra is also the chakra of interpersonal relationships. It's your personality—what you say (and don't say) in this world, how you act out, behave, and react to the world around you. If the third chakra is blocked, which is what happens to cause a Masochistic defense to form, it cannot work with the creative energy. This is often how a person's Core Essence gets blocked.

When parents are controlling, a distortion (or a block) in a child's third chakra can form. Most parents don't even realize that they are controlling. Too much control forces a child to submit to the Will of the parent. This means the child's Will is held back. They don't get to do what they desire; they do what they are told. This cycle suppresses creative energy, causing it to become backed up in the third chakra. It has nowhere to go so it winds up cycling and cycling within the person's Energy Field. Often people who are using the Masochist defense are overweight even if they don't eat that much. Their Energy Field is heavy and sluggish because of the recycled creative energy, causing the physical body to become heavy, sluggish and tired. These people often complain of fatigue and an overall lack of energy and enthusiasm for life.

People can develop autoimmune diseases from this defense. Some examples of autoimmune diseases are Systemic Lupus, Fibromyalgia, Rheumatoid Arthritis and Chronic Fatigue Syndrome. Autoimmune means "self attack" and that is exactly what is happening. The body is attacking itself because the creative energy is being pushed back into the body. Creative energy normally flows outward, but when someone is in this defense the energy cycles in on itself and becomes trapped inside the Energy Field. It never gets to go out and be used. In other words, the person has feelings and opinions that they don't get to express.

This is why Masochistic people have the least amount of awareness as to who they truly are. Since creative energy is life force (which is the energy that comes directly from the Core Essence) and life force is *awareness,* if it is blocked, you lose conscious awareness of yourself. You become numb. By the time they're an adult, Masochists take up where their parents left off and control themselves. They suppress their own individual awareness and are only conscious of what other people tell them. Just as when they were children, they do as they're told and hold back their own opinions and desires. Most Masochists don't even realize that they are suppressing themselves because by the time they are an adult, suppression seems natural to them. In other words, they're not aware that they're not aware!

What this sets up is a person who endures life instead of creating their own life. The Masochist lets other people tell them what to do and allows other people to control them. They rarely, if ever, give their own opinion or tell a story that is unique to them. When you ask them where they want to go for dinner, they'll often say "wherever you want to go is fine."

The Masochist appears very nice at first glance. They are usually a bit overweight with a round face and good-natured. At a deeper level they are actually filled with rage and shame. The rage comes from holding themselves back and always giving into other people, never really expressing themselves. Creative energy has a lot of charge to it, so when it is held in, it causes a lot of suppressed rage. This is because the energy was meant to flow out but it got twisted inwards instead. The energy forms anger as it twists back inward. How many times have you wanted to say something to someone but held back and then later kept thinking about what you *should* have said or done? There is always anger when we are not allowed to express, because expression is a person's natural state of being. It is unnatural to hold yourself back.

The shame is the hidden belief that they are not good enough. The Masochist is someone who endured being controlled and told what to do as a child. This is what created shameful feelings of "not being good enough." Underneath their pleasant facade is a fear that if they were good enough to begin with, they would have been allowed to express themselves. They assume that because the controlling parent was always telling them what to do, that what they wanted to do was not good enough. They also assume that because the parent had to come in and tell them exactly how to clean the room and where to put everything, that they are too "stupid" to have done it on their own. Many times they are even told this. Now they have to live in a bedroom where everything is not where they want it to be, but where the parent wants it to be. They lose confidence in themselves and shame develops about their own individual opinions and feelings.

When the Masochist was a small child the parent constantly told the child what to do and usually how to do it. This child had very little to no input in their own life. They were told what to wear, what to eat, how to study, how to play, what to play, what they could or could not tell their friends, what to watch on TV, how to act and so on. A conflict arises because the child is so angry at the controlling parent but is afraid to hate the parent because they just want to be held and loved so much. Shame is born out of this also. Shame at hating the parent and shame at holding themselves back.

The biggest problem with the Masochist defense is that it keeps a person in complete denial. This is the person that will say they had no problems in childhood. They are usually in unhealthy relationships yet they will tell you that everything is fine. They are usually in jobs that are not a good match for their natural abilities but because they are not aware of what their natural abilities are, they see nothing wrong with their job. They often stay in the same repetitive job for a long time. Their energy is trapped, so they become trapped. They have a hard time seeing that there are any issues at all. Whenever a person takes drugs that depress their system, like valium or sleeping pills, they are increasing this level of their Shadow. Alcohol is probably the most common depressant used. The Masochist is built on the premise of denial, specifically denial of a person's individual personality, and depressants keep a person in that denial. It's important for these people to stop numbing themselves externally and allow their lack of awareness and energy to be felt.

The Masochist has a very naïve nature. The defense keeps them this way so they don't start looking at their lives or themselves. It does not matter how much formal education they have, the defense keeps them from thinking for themselves or forming their own opinions to keep them in a naïve place. This is the Shadow's first line of defense and it is usually a strong one.

This characterology likes to keep the person in group mentality to avoid allowing them to think for themselves. In a group setting, the Masochist will look to whomever they perceive as the authority and go along with that person's opinion. The Masochist loves to be either completely alone (so no one can control them) or blended into a group. What they don't like is if they have to participate individually. They don't mind helping write the lecture but they don't want to have to get up and give it. They don't mind speaking out if everyone else is speaking out, but they don't want to speak out alone or have to give their own opinion. If they do have to speak out in a group, they often repeat what someone else just said or they quote something they just read. Either way they don't realize that they did not express their *own* opinion. They take other people's opinions and make them their own. This is what's known as blending. Masochists blend themselves in with the crowd to avoid being seen or heard. This is also the way they avoid thinking for themselves. And because they are in such strong denial, they don't see that their "opinion" is really a copy of someone else's. This is the person in a group that is always asking everyone else what their opinions are, how other people are going to vote, what other people want to do and so on. Then they mimic what everyone else's answers are.

The Masochist is perpetually looking for a parent figure to tell them what to do. They have a very hard time when they don't know what to do, because this challenges them to come up with their own answers. The Masochist does not want to come up with their own answers because their own opinions are covered in so much shame. They just want to follow directions and be told what to do. They usually marry very controlling people who love telling them what to do. This re-creates their controlling childhood.

The Masochistic defense works by caving in the third chakra. This prevents the person from really connecting in relationships and from having an individual personality. What this means is that the Masochist does not relate well to others. On the surface they do, but this is because they agree with everyone around them and do whatever they are told. They were trained this way in their childhood. But this is not a healthy, connected way to relate to people. This is like a robot just following orders. Deep inside there is a hidden rage at their inability to express for themselves.

The outward action of the Masochist is very passive but inwardly they are angry at being controlled. This is the defense that created passive/aggressive behavior. What they don't realize is that they are the ones doing the controlling by holding themselves in. They held back so much in their childhood that it became instinctual for them to hold back as an adult. It became normal to be passive. They are re-creating the trapped feeling they had in childhood. *Ultimately, their anger is really at themselves for holding themselves hostage.* They want out; they just don't remember how to get out.

The power in the Masochist characterology increases when people do not stop and question their choices and/or behavior. Take the time to look at why you do what you do and you will begin to see your patterns. This will start to dissolve the Masochist layer of your Defense System and challenge you to stop being in denial. You have nothing to be ashamed of. The Masochist defense counts on the fact that you stay numb and don't question anything. Start questioning and you will start dissolving your numbness. Awareness is real power; the less awareness you have, the less real empowerment you have. And if you're not using your power, then your Shadow Self is!

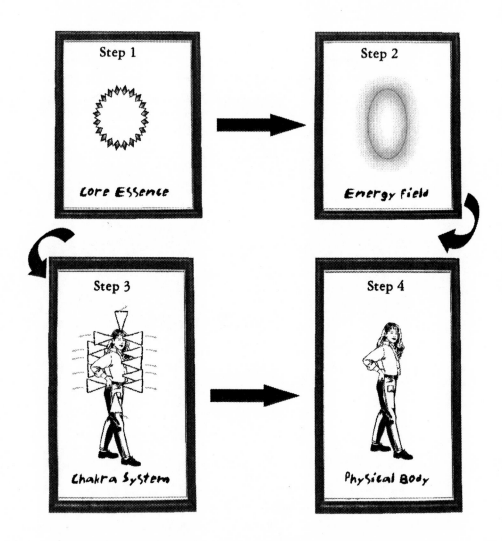

Information flows from the Core Essence level to the Energy Field, then to the Chakra System and into the Physical Body. The process works in reverse, the Physical Body sends messages through the Chakra System into the Energy Field and the Core Essence level.

CHAPTER SEVENTEEN

The Energy System

The Energy System consists of the *physical body*, the *Chakra System* and the *Energy Field*. All three work together, functioning both independently and as one unit. This concept was introduced earlier when talking about the physical body. The physical body is made up of 11 different systems (like the cardiovascular system and the nervous system) with each system functioning independently yet at the same time, functioning as part of a whole.

In the physical body, information is processed by the brain and then passed along to the rest of the body through the nervous system and the endocrine system. The nervous system sends messages up and down the spinal column, then out through the hundreds of thousands of individual nerves that branch off and go throughout the body. The endocrine system sends information through hormones to all of the major glands in the body like the thyroid, ovaries and pancreas, where the messages are then spread throughout the rest of the body along with chemicals that help the body adjust and change. Information does not necessarily originate in the brain; it's simply processed there. For example, you can get a cut on your finger and it will be the nerves and cells directly affected by the cut that originate the information and then send off the message to the brain. The brain's job is to have a comprehensive overview of what is going on throughout the whole body and act accordingly.

Message sending is a two-way street. Some messages originate in the physical dimension where they start in the physical body then go into the Chakra System and through the Energy Field where the information is sent along to the Core Essence level. The Core Essence sends its own messages through the reverse process; messages go from the Core Essence to the Energy Field, into the Chakra System and then to the physical body. It's the ultimate information highway! It is also a very complex system that's affected by all the choices a person makes in their life and the pre-existing circumstances they set up to help them learn, change or grow from a soul perspective.

For example, on a soul level a person may be growing and learning about parenting so they will have patterns set up in their Energy Field that will propel them to become a parent and raise children. From the second you are born, you have free will. Nothing is completely pre-determined. Life is made up as you go, but everyone does have traits and patterns that are in their Energy Field to create environments that reflect whatever a person is working on during their lifetime.

This is similar to the concept of astrology, which defines people as having personal traits related by birth signs. For example, Capricorns have the trait of being organized. This does not mean that every Capricorn is organized; it just means that they have a natural aptitude for being organized. On a soul level, a person may be born under the astrological sign of Capricorn because they are learning to be more organized. In this example the person will have a life that challenges them into becoming more proficient at being organized. Another soul may choose to be born under the sign of Capricorn because they need to be organized to accomplish another goal they have for themselves. For this person, being organized will be second nature and they will not find it challenging at all. It will seem natural.

Your whole Energy System is one big message center. It holds information that helps to create your lifetime, and it continually sends messages back and forth between the spiritual and physical realms, even when you are sleeping. Healing is not about "fixing" or "changing" your chakras or your Energy Field. **Healing is about self-understanding, self-exploration and growth.** This is done by learning to communicate with *yourself.* The Chakra System, the Energy Field and your physical body are all just messengers that help you through this process of self-understanding. What messages are you sending to your soul and what messages are you receiving?

   Your life and your Energy System are one and the same. Your life is a reflection of what is going on within you. All change comes from exploring your inner reality first. Your outer reality will shift and change to reflect that inner reality.

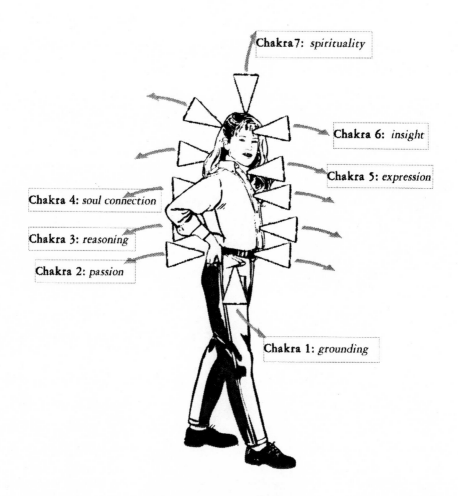

Chakra 7: *spirituality*

Chakra 6: *insight*

Chakra 5: *expression*

Chakra 4: *soul connection*

Chakra 3: *reasoning*

Chakra 2: *passion*

Chakra 1: *grounding*

THE 7-BASIC CHAKRAS

Will Centers

Emotional Centers

CHAPTER EIGHTEEN

The Chakra System

There are seven main chakras that connect into the physical body. Each chakra is in a specific area and has specific job requirements. The chakras are numbered 1-7. The first chakra sits in the groin area, the second chakra is around the bladder, the third chakra sits where the stomach is, the fourth is at the heart, the fifth is in the throat, the sixth in the forehead and the seventh is at the top, or crown, of the head. When they are healthy, each chakra is the same size.

Energy from the first chakra comes out of the groin area going downward to the earth. Energy from the seventh chakra comes out of the top of the head and goes towards the sky. They represent the connection between "heaven" and "earth." The chakras in between, 2-6, all have front and back chakras. Both the front and back chakras look the same but process different information. The back chakras are known as the *Will Centers* and the front chakras are the *Emotional Centers*.

A person's Will is the combination of a person's choice and inclination to do (or not do) something, so the back of the chakras send out information regarding how much Will a person is putting into something and the front chakras send out how much emotion a person has in what they are doing. For example, a person could be comfortably lying on their couch watching TV during a rainstorm, but they have a craving for ice-cream and are in the process of deciding whether they really want to go out into the storm to get the ice-cream. How much desire they have for the ice-cream (emotion) and how much they are willing to get up and go out into the storm to get the ice-cream will determine the outcome. Only when the Will Centers and Emotional Centers are balanced is the outcome of any decision-making process in harmony.

The overall job of each chakra is to translate and send messages between the physical body and the Energy Field. This is a very complex job. Any distortion in a chakra will create distortions in both the incoming and outgoing messages.

The chakras are a great place to learn about the different dimensions that make up a person. Each chakra represents a dimension, or a state of being, in a person. Culturally they also represent the dimensional levels Mankind has evolved from, and is evolving towards. For example the first chakra deals with basic physical survival and represents the time period when Man was in a more barbaric state which would now be referred to as Neanderthal. This was a period when neither the mind nor emotions were evolved and everyday life focused on survival. As Man did evolve and became more group orientated, the world itself gradually evolved out of the first dimension and went into the second dimension which also represents the exploration of the second chakra. This chakra deals with emotions, creativity, passion, art, music, poetry and sex just to name a few traits. Historically, this included the rise and fall of the Greek empire, the Regency period and the Renaissance, all of which focused on passion and artistic ability. Great authors and artists came out of this era along with a lot of sexual exploitation and violence. The violence in this era was not about survival; it was more about who had the most to gain and who could emotionally (and sexually) manipulate better. These are very second chakra traits.

Today the world is in the third dimension working its way towards the fourth. The third dimension is an exploration into the third chakra which encompasses things like interpersonal relationships, technology, mental thought, linear thinking, right/wrong, ethics, personal power and manipulation of power. The third chakra has a lot to do with the separation between the mind of Man (ego) which explores only that which it can see and feel, and the heart of

God. "Prove it to me" could be a motto for the third dimension which is all about personal power versus empowerment through spiritual connection (hint … that's the fourth dimension!).

When you're working with the concept of dimensions, part of what you're working with are levels of consciousness. As an example, you can think of your five basic senses as five different "dimensions." When you are focusing on hearing something, you are in the "hearing dimension," and when you are focused on seeing something, you are in the "sight dimension." In reality, when you are experiencing anything you are experiencing it with multiple senses, multiple "dimensions" all at the same time. However, there are times, like when you are in a movie theatre, that you use some senses more dominantly than others, like hearing and sight versus smell and touch. People usually don't focus on one of their senses unless something is wrong, like their eyesight is diminishing. Then they realize they have a problem and start working with the "sight dimension."

The Chakra System works with the same principle with each chakra literally in a different dimension. On a daily basis people use all seven chakras, all seven dimensions, at the same time. The information in each chakra flows into the Energy Field where one solid reality, your life, is formed. This is where the concept of dimensions becomes very important. If a person is going to be "in the moment," which means they are grounded and present within themselves, then they have to be present with the overall vibration in their Energy Field. Each chakra functions at a certain vibration, like a sound wave. The lower chakras are very dense, like the lower notes on a piano. The upper chakras are very high pitched, like a dog whistle. When the chakras send all their messages into the Energy Field, the Energy Field takes on a singular vibration. This means that even though each chakra is in its own dimension, **the chakras function collectively in one dimension**. As a person evolves, they clear out the issues in their chakras raising the individual vibration of each chakra. This increases the overall vibration in their Energy Field and eventually takes that person into a higher dimension. This process is known as *ascension*. A person ascends from the second dimension into the third, from the third into the fourth and so on.

Since the overall consciousness on the planet is in the third dimension, this means that the average vibration of everyone's Energy Field is in the third dimension.

Even though the collective consciousness is in the third dimension, it does not mean that every individual is, just the majority. There are plenty of people still functioning in the second dimension and there are some people functioning from higher dimensions than the third.

When a person meditates or spends a lot of time in prayer, their consciousness leaves the limitation of the third dimension and can expand to very high dimensions and vibrations. No matter what dimension someone reaches in a meditative state, when their consciousness comes back into their physical body, they come back to whatever dimensional state, or vibration, that they function from *in this reality.* In other words, whatever vibration their Energy Field is at in the present time. This is an important distinction. Many people have told me they want to live from the same place they find when they meditate, which is a more peaceful, calm and fluid state than what they find when they are consciously in their bodies. This is a beautiful goal and one that is very attainable, but a person has to start from whatever place their Energy Field is in right *now.* Enlightenment is not about getting out of your body and living from some higher dimension; it's about dealing with who, what and where you are right now. In other words, if you want to learn all about yourself, generally speaking, starting at the seventh chakra (which is the chakra of spiritual connection) is not going to get you there. You need to look at all of your chakras, all of yourself, and be realistic as to where you are in this moment. It's great to have an experience of inner peace and say "hey, I want to live like that all the time," but realistically, to achieve that goal you have to come back down to reality, let go of the Idealized Self-Image and deal with wherever your overall consciousness is right now. If you're angry, be angry. If you're numb, be numb. Use these as starting places to help you find the things that hold you back from being in inner peace. *There's no jumping ahead when it comes to enlightenment.* You have to stop and deal with what is going on inside of you, and it's your Chakra System that breaks down, and stores your Shadow-based issues in specific places in your body.

Any true healing, or spiritual growth, is a journey. It is not about going into higher states of consciousness and staying there. Remember, you are your Shadow Self as well as your Core Essence. It is only when aspects of your Shadow Self are discovered and shifted back into the Core Essence that your whole vibration increases. This is how a person's whole being shifts from one dimensional state into another. If you take your consciousness into a higher dimension through a method like meditation, then yes, that part of your consciousness is now more enlightened, but what about the rest of you? What about the unconscious part of you? You, as a whole, are not enlightened. Just the part of your consciousness that went off into the higher dimension! Spending too much time in higher vibrations can cause a greater and greater gap between what you think is reality and what really is reality. I once had someone tell me, "I do yoga every day so there is nothing wrong with me; I'm completely enlightened." I have also heard similar statements from people telling me how much they meditate, therefore they must be all light by now. Exploration is a great way to show yourself that you can increase your vibration, but you have to work at shifting where you are at now to where you want to be. You can't grow in anything if you can't be real with where you are right now.

I talk about this here because over the past few years I have met many people who talk about how they are "in" as much as the 5th or 6th dimension. They may be "in" those dimensions in a Schizoid or meditative state of consciousness, but they weren't in either of those dimensions in this reality when I met them. The fourth dimension is *unconditional love*. If you were in this state, you would never be abusive or harm another individual. This means not even with your thoughts! If you were coming from the sixth dimension, you would be incapable of having a negative thought about yourself or another. As you can see by looking around, this planet has a ways to go. It is easy to get caught up in spiritual ego and believe that you are more advanced than you are. Yes, there are people walking around on this planet that are in the 4th, 5th and 6th dimensions, but it is very rare and I guarantee they are not calling themselves "Masters" or walking around talking about what dimension they function from.

Every time a person elevates their consciousness level to higher states in meditation, they are bringing a piece of that higher vibration back with them. When someone truly hits the "zone" in a meditative state, they are at least in the fourth dimension while meditating. This is why they feel so calm and peaceful when their consciousness first comes back into their body from the meditative state. Meditating is one way a person increases their overall vibration, awareness and enlightenment. Meditation is only part of the puzzle. It is the willingness to look at yourself, the good and bad, that increases your awareness allowing you to consciously access more and more of your Essence.

Spiritual growth is not some race. You don't need to get anywhere. You're exactly where you need to be. You're okay just as you are. In school, 4th grade is not better than 3rd grade. It's just 4th grade. If you're alive on this planet right now you have some work to do in the third dimension. This does not mean that you are necessarily working on your third chakra, just that you are doing some work, somewhere, in the third dimension. Remember, a dimension is just a state of being. You can think of water, air and fire as three different dimensions. If you put your right arm in water and move it around, you will get a different experience than if you put your right arm in fire or air and move it around. As a soul, we experience everything in every dimension. Life is not about getting to the next dimension; it's about being present with, and experiencing everything from whatever vibrational level your Chakra System is in right now. Part of the reason we experience life at different dimensions is so we can have the same experience from different angles, just like the above example of putting your arm in water versus fire. For example, if you were watching an action movie from the first or third dimensions, there would be feelings of aggression and the chemicals in your body that deal with aggression would be higher. If you were watching the same movie from the fourth or seventh dimension, it would be a very painful experience as you would feel the pain of the violence as if it were really happening to you.

All of your chakras work together and feed the collective information into whatever level your particular Energy Field is functioning from. Each chakra does have a unique job and a unique interpretation to add to the Energy Field, but the chakras do function as one overall unit. This is similar to the physical body which is made up of many different organs like the lungs, liver and heart, yet they all work together as one unit—your body. As a whole, your soul along with everyone else's is on a journey of evolution and growth. At this particular time, on this particular planet, the evolution is about moving from the third dimension into the fourth. It is the individual chakras that are the tools for this growth.

Energy enters the Chakra System from the seventh chakra going downward to the first chakra, and then turns around and comes back up and out the seventh. (There are more than seven chakras, but the first seven chakras are the basic chakras used in this physical existence. If you go further out of the body, the Chakra System starts dealing with soul connections and soul groups. For the purposes of this book, I'll stay with the chakras that most affect the conscious awareness at this time.) As the energy goes downward a person can feel their connection to spirit, as it goes upwards they can feel their connection to themselves. The energy winds in and out of each chakra causing a spiral effect. Each chakra is in charge of a certain area of the body and is responsible for the physical, mental, emotional and spiritual levels in their area. An example of this would be the fourth chakra. It sits in the middle of your chest right where the breast bone is. It is responsible for the heart, lungs, ribs and shoulders just to name a few physical aspects. It is also responsible for things like soul connection, grief, bitterness, unconditional love, joy and peace.

When describing what a chakra looks like, you need to take into consideration what dimension you are looking at. This is because the Chakra System looks different depending on which dimension you're coming from and which dimension you look at. Many pictures that I have seen depicting a chakra show a cone-shaped object with light beams, or small inner circular areas of light coming from the cone. To me, this is similar to what a chakra looks like in the third dimension, and since the overall planetary consciousness is in the third dimension, most people probably do perceive chakras to look like this.

When I look at a chakra from the perspective of the first dimension, I see an object that looks similar to a hockey puck, rounded and dense. When I look at a chakra from the perspective of the second dimension, I see something totally different. When I look from the third dimension, I do see a cone-shaped object but to me it really looks more like a small fast moving vortex. A tornado is good example of a large moving vortex. A tornado is really just wind moving in a fast spiral pattern, and when I look at a chakra from the third dimension, I see light beams moving in a fast spiral pattern that when seen as a whole, looks like a cone.

When looking at the Chakra System, I see seven different shapes for the seven different dimensions. In each dimension all of the chakras have the same shape. So when I look at the Chakra System from the first dimension, I see seven chakras that resemble hockey pucks. When I look at the Chakra System from the third dimension, I see seven different cone shapes that resemble mini tornados. When the planet as a whole is living more from the fourth dimension, the Chakra System as a whole will probably be described as being more spherically shaped because in the fourth dimension this is what chakras look like. This is an important concept in regards to learning about working with chakras, because everyone will perceive a chakra uniquely. It just depends on what level they are coming from. Just because one person describes a chakra in one form and another person in another form does not necessarily make either of them wrong. They're probably seeing the same chakra from different places.

Within the Chakra System, each chakra has its own vibration and its own color. The lower chakras are very dense, so the sound is low in pitch and darker in color. As you go upward in the Chakra System, the sound becomes higher in pitch and the color becomes lighter and brighter. Each chakra is a complex system of grids and light beams. The light beams work similar to the electrical wiring inside a house where the electricity is sent via the wires. This is how the energetic messages get sent in and out of chakras. The light beams function like wiring and are used as the transportation system for the actual messages. The grids are similar to computer chips. They hold all the information that a chakra has available at any given time. These grids get updated by a person's Core Essence when things change, like when a belief gets released, a wound becomes healed or some aspect of a person's False Self is shifted.

The grids that make up the chakras are templates. Templates are like blueprints. When you take a photograph with one of those cameras that gives you a picture that develops in a few moments, the picture comes out of the camera looking like a gray mass. The gray area is sticky due to the developing fluid in it but within moments a picture forms out of the gray mass. The "gray mass" is a template and from this, a solid picture is created. The picture was there the whole time; it was just in the process of being developed. The templates in your chakras work on the same principle. The templates hold the information inside each chakra and then send that information out into your Energy Field. Each chakra holds its own template, or blueprint, and then all seven of the chakras send their information into the Energy Field creating one big template.

For example, the fourth chakra is the chakra of unconditional love. A person's soul could be working on issues of unconditional love, specifically giving love without expectation. The fourth chakra will reflect this in the person's life. The chakra will develop a template for this concept and then pass it on to the Energy Field where it will be added to all of the other templates. It is the Energy Field that is the overall template, or blueprint, for a person's actual life. When a chakra sends out a message to the Energy Field, that "message" becomes a reality for that person. In this example, the fourth chakra could be sending out a message that brings people forth that need love, but never return love. This could be one potential way a soul uses to learn and grow in the art of giving unconditional love.

Because each chakra is made up of a compilation of different energies, it is not really a solid object and does not really have just one color. Chakras are constantly in flux, but when seen as a whole object they do tend to have an overall color to them. It's like the sky. The sky is not really blue, but when seen from a distance as a whole object, on a sunny day the overall color of the sky does look blue. In general, from the perspective of the third dimension the first chakra looks red, the second chakra appears orange, the third is yellow, the fourth is green, the fifth is blue, the sixth is indigo and the seventh is white. The following is a more specific look at the overall traits of each chakra.

FIRST CHAKRA

This chakra deals with the physical foundation for the body. How healthy and strong the body is directly relates to how healthy this chakra is. When someone is born with an abnormality or becomes extremely ill in the first year of life, generally speaking they were born with a distortion already present in this chakra. Grounding, trust, safety, and security rule this chakra. It is the area of basic survival. How safe a person feels in the world, or even in their own home, and how much trust a person has represents the degree of health in this chakra. The first chakra is easily distorted when a person grows up in a household where they do not feel safe as an infant. This chakra is most vulnerable from conception–twelve months old. It can be distorted by physical violence in the house, a mother not wanting the baby, sexual abuse, physical abuse and neglect just to name a few of the most common examples.

The first chakra governs a person's adrenal glands. The adrenal glands regulate the hormones that are released whenever the body senses danger, like adrenaline. When adrenaline is released into the bloodstream, it gives the body a kick, like caffeine does. Along with this kick a person can get the distorted feeling that they can handle anything. This is usually an illusion. When running from a mugger this can come in handy, but most often this is not what people use their adrenaline for. A lot of the time people just do not feel safe and trusting within their own bodies (this is because their first chakra doesn't have a strong connection to their Higher Self) causing a part of themselves to be living in fear every day. This fear often takes the form of anxiety, difficulty sleeping, a strong Idealized Self-Image (overcompensation,) or a short-temper. The fear alerts the adrenal glands which then send out a low level of adrenaline and "poof" suddenly the person feels like they are okay. The problem is that this is a *false sense* of okay. Many peoples' False Image starts right here. They develop a false sense of power by the low level of adrenaline running around their body and it creates a distorted ego. Adrenaline is a natural high, it makes you feel and see things in a distorted way, so it is easy for the negative ego to take this chemical and make your consciousness believe that you are safer, smarter, stronger and just generally in a more advanced place than the reality of where you're really at. Ironically, the more adrenaline a person runs, the more unsafe they really are because of the distorted sense of awareness that accompanies the rush. The concept of tunnel vision comes out of here, the mind becomes hyper-aware of the one thing that is causing fear/anxiety and completely unaware of everything else around them.

Many people have told me "I can't meditate, my mind won't slow down." Meditation is directly related to the first chakra. Meditation is the art of letting go of the mind and allowing spiritual consciousness to come in. If a person does not feel safe, they are a lot less likely to let go and allow something to open up within them that they feel like they can't control. And God is something you definitely can't control!

I would suggest to everyone to keep trying to meditate because it is in the act of allowing your spirit to open up into the physical body that the first chakra will heal. If the first chakra is distorted in any way, then you do not trust or feel safe in this world. It is in reconnecting to your spirit that the first chakra will start to remember that it's part of a larger Being and that you are okay. The more disconnected this chakra is, the more a person is likely to have anxiety disorders, allergies (which is a rejection of the physical world around you) and have a tendency to give over personal power in a hope that other people will keep you safe. But any "safety" found outside of yourself is a false sense of security. Real safety and security comes from within and this requires trust. I've never met a person who did not have issues with trust, but ultimately any issue with trust is within you. *Your trust in this world is directly related to how much you trust yourself.* The more energy a person has coming in from their Core Essence and filling up their first chakra, the more they will trust themselves and the world around them.

SECOND CHAKRA

This chakra is the emotional foundation for the body. Passion, emotion, sexuality, inner gifts and nurturing come from here. Passion is not just about sex; passion is how much pizzazz you feel about anything! How much do you love your job? Your personal life? What beliefs would you die for? Live for? How much do you really want something? This is passion. It's pure creative energy. Often aggression and revenge are mistaken for passion. True passion does not actively harm; it is creative life force, not destructive action.

The first chakra deals with physical safety, but it is the second chakra that deals with emotional safety. Both of these chakras form the foundation for a person's body. Both of these chakras feed energy to the pelvis, legs and feet. Getting your "legs knocked out from underneath you" is a literal term in energy work. You can physically have your legs knocked out from under you or emotionally have your legs knocked out from under you. Whenever someone has a severe emotional shock, they usually have to sit down. This is because an emotional shock is similar to a physical blow to the pelvic area; it distorts the second chakra which then limits how much energy can flow down a person's legs.

The second chakra sits in the area where the bladder is down in the lower pelvis. This area is where nurturing enters the body. If a person does not receive healthy nurturing as a child, they generally will not develop a healthy second chakra. This leads to an adult who either manipulates to get nurturing, abusively takes nurturing, or over nurtures other people in hopes that they'll get attention in return. This chakra is also referred to as the "inner child." This is because the consciousness level in this chakra is often wounded in early childhood right around the "me me me" stage which is about eighteen months to three years old. As an adult, a distorted second chakra can be easy to see because the adult behavior is very selfish, self-centered and childlike. This is the adult who is always looking for someone else to do their work, to meet their emotional needs, to get reassurance from or to blame.

Obsessive disorders come from this chakra. In a healthy state, this chakra gives a person the feeling of being full and nurtured. When this does not happen, a person feels empty in some way. Drugs, alcohol and food are common ways people feed this urge to be "fulfilled." Obsessive thoughts and actions are another way. The mind either numbs the person out (drugs/food) or keeps them busy thinking/doing something all the time to avoid feeling the loneliness and pain of not being nurtured.

Along with the bladder this chakra also governs the large bowel. The more unfulfilled a person is, the more they do not nurture themselves or allow the joy of life into their world the more constipated, inflamed and/or irregular a person's bowels will function.

The old saying "looking for love in all the wrong places" was made for this chakra. Often people will use sex to replace their lack of self-nurturing. When people feel empty in this area they crave attention. They can become fixated with finding a partner with the unconscious hope that the other person will meet their needs by filling up the part of them that feels needy, unloved and unheard. Many people really do marry partners who carry the traits of their parents in hopes that the parental needs that didn't get met as a child will be met by their spouse. This puts a lot of projection and expectation onto the spouse, hence the very high divorce rate. I once had a client that had close to fifty lovers by the time they were thirty years old, and they weren't a prostitute. They did not see anything unusual about their sex life, believing that "normal" people sought out multiple sexual partners. Sex is rarely an issue itself; it is often a reflection of emotional neediness. Someone who has multiple sexual partners has an inner-child screaming for attention. Working with this chakra means working with your unfulfilled emotional needs.

THIRD CHAKRA

The third chakra is the foundation for a person's relationships, both with themselves and the world around them. This chakra takes all of the messages it gets from the first and second chakras, and then combines that information to create a plan of action. The first chakra sends information about what the physical body is feeling (like tired, hurt, cold, strong, etc.) along with information about the surrounding environment. For example, a person goes to a party and walks in by themselves; the first chakra lets the person know if they feel safe, scared, cold, or hot and if they recognize anyone standing around them. The second chakra adds emotion to this information along with how much passion and desire they have about being at the party. It can also sense the overall state of emotion going on at the party. It's the third chakra that puts it all together through the process of logical and rational thought. It takes the raw physical data from the first chakra, adds the emotional data from the second chakra and makes choices based on the information it receives. In this example, if the person feels happy and safe because they recognize a bunch of people they know, the third chakra may decide to be social and go talk to these people, maybe even eat some snacks or have a drink. If the data was different, maybe the first chakra sends a message saying that it doesn't feel safe and the second chakra doesn't send out much passion, the third chakra may decide to go home, go in a corner or try a forced approach to socializing.

The third chakra is basically a person's personality. At the level of being a child the personality is something to be nurtured, coaxed out and given space to grow. Many children grow up in environments where the parents force their Will, their personality, onto the child. If the parents love to eat meat, then they often teach their children that they "have to" eat meat. When things like this happen, a child often gets a distortion in their third chakra making their personality more about what they learn rather than who they really are. This creates a False Image. *Part of the healing journey is to find out who you were before your environment taught you who you were.* If no one ever trained you to think in certain patterns, who would you Be? This answer lies in the third chakra.

Physiologically this chakra controls gastrointestinal organs like the stomach, spleen, gall bladder, liver, pancreas and small bowel. By the amount of diagnosed diseases related to these organs like stomach ulcers, food allergies, diabetes, gall stones and indigestion it is easy to see that culturally we have an issue of over-controlling children. Children are not brought into this world to be "trained," they are here to grow in themselves, and that is a big distinction.

FOURTH CHAKRA

The fourth chakra is the foundation for unconditional love. It has a challenging job because it has to mediate the primal desires and unmet needs felt in the lower chakras with the Higher purpose and larger picture that is found in the upper chakras. "Heart & Soul" is a term that has been used in countless songs and many beautiful works of poetry. There is a reason why—they truly are connected. This is the first chakra that is *consciously* connected into a person's soul level.

The first three chakras focus on a person's individualism. They focus on the experience of being separated. The heart chakra is the first chakra (in succession) that deals with experiencing yourself as part of larger picture. It is the first dimension that takes the consciousness beyond the individuated Self and connects it into the group consciousness of God. When a person is coming from their heart chakra, their awareness comes from the fourth dimension. At this dimension, if you said a derogatory comment or had a negative thought about another person, your heart area would actually hurt. Other people's pain becomes something you experience, especially if you are the cause of that pain. It is at this level of evolution that peace and harmony become the "normal" choices. To harm another is to literally harm thyself, and it is only when you are coming from your heart that you can feel this.

Many people consider themselves very "sensitive" and talk about how they can "feel" other people's pain. This does not necessarily mean that they are coming from their heart, let alone the fourth dimension. Your Chakra System is like your physical body, it only stays healthy if everything is in balance. When a person's heart chakra is in balance, it can feel the pain of the planet as well as an individual person's pain but the pain *runs* through the chakra, it does not stay. Often when I see the Energy Field of someone who is complaining of being "too sensitive" and feeling "everyone else's pain," I see that what they are really feeling is a reflection of their own (held) pain. For example, a person has unresolved grief over their own father's death and then visits a friend who just lost their father. They start experiencing feelings of grief and pain but believe that they are feeling their friend's pain when what they are really feeling is their own incomplete grieving process. If they were coming from their heart, they would not be *in* grief and pain; they would simply feel it running through them. There is a big difference between experiencing something running through you and being in the process of experiencing something for yourself.

This chakra works with a person's lungs, heart, blood flow, thymus and immune system. Physiologically and energetically this chakra works with maintaining balance throughout the whole body. There is an old saying about "getting to the heart of the matter" which refers to getting right down into the original place, or issue, something started out from. Finding out what the original source is. This means getting to the soul level. Understanding the origin of any problem or illness a person has would definitely require connecting to their soul level, as no one knows you better than your own soul.

A good healer works from this level at all times. It is the heart chakra that, on a technical level, transmutes Lower Self consciousness into Higher Self consciousness. The heart chakra is the major tool used in healing. It is a great place to start if you are working on healing yourself. You can go into this chakra to connect to your Higher Self and spiritual guardian to help you understand your True Self and your higher purpose. This is also why the training period for healers can be so long, because every time they open their heart chakra to work on someone else, they can become triggered by their own unresolved issues. The heart feels everything, so it is through the process of self-examination and healing that healers are born. The more a healer works on themselves, the deeper into their own issues they can go, so the deeper into their own heart chakra they then work from. The deeper a healer can go into their own heart chakra, the more affective they are in a healing. The deeper anyone can go into their heart chakra, the more joy, love, compassion and peace they will live from.

FIFTH CHAKRA

This chakra is the foundation for expression. Your ability to communicate with anything, and this includes receiving messages as well as sending them, relies on this chakra. The throat, mouth, teeth, jaw, gums and ears are part of this chakra. By the amount of teeth problems, throat infections, hearing loss and jaw problems, you can see that there is an overall issue with expression in this world.

It's important to understand that just because someone frequently speaks out does not mean that their fifth chakra is clear, and in the reverse just because someone is quiet does not mean that this chakra is distorted. Expression comes in many forms and speech is just one of them. Movement, dance, singing, writing, painting, film-making, listening, reading and meditating are just a few methods of expressing and receiving information.

Another important thing to know about this chakra is that it can learn to express anything, but this doesn't mean that what a person is expressing is personal Truth. The chakra will express whatever it is told to express, so if you are coming from your Core Essence, then that's what the chakra expresses. If you're coming from your Shadow Self, then that's what you're putting out.

This chakra is the place where a person learns to speak their Truth versus what they have been taught. All chakras, when in their natural form, will come from Truth. It is in the fifth chakra that a person's Will decides what they are, or are not, going to do—follow their Higher Self or their Lower Self. When the chakra is used to hold back personal Truth, then a person is holding themselves back. For example, let's say you're in a movie theatre and halfway through the show you have to use the bathroom but you're sitting in the middle of a row and you don't want to get up, because you don't want to disturb the other people in the theatre. In this scenario, you have just chosen **not** to express yourself by not getting up and meeting your own physical needs. Movement is expression. In this example, you have just used your fifth chakra to increase your Victim Consciousness and decrease your self-worth by holding yourself back and not expressing your need.

The fifth chakra is probably the most common chakra that people use to hold themselves back. Instead of speaking out a personal opinion, a need or an original idea, many people use this chakra to conform to group mentality and group consciousness. People will speak out all the time from this chakra; they're just not speaking from their True Self but rather from their Shadow Self.

If the first three chakras are not well developed, it's hard to have a healthy fifth chakra. This is because the third chakra is the area that develops an individual personality and the fifth chakra is the area that expresses that individual personality, so if the third chakra is not healthy, the fifth chakra does not have anything healthy to express. And if the first two chakras are not in light, the person will not be comfortable or feel safe; it is more likely that they will concede their personal expression for another person's (or group's) desires.

To work with the fifth chakra is to work with expressing your True Self. This requires that a person identify and release their learned behaviors, beliefs and training so that they can express from their Core Essence.

SIXTH CHAKRA

This chakra is the foundation for insight. Insight means "within sight." In other words, this chakra is about what you're really seeing versus what you think you are seeing. The sixth chakra is often referred to as the "third eye." Physiologically the sixth chakra works with the pineal gland, brain, sinuses and eyes.

Your physical eyes are actually a very complex system. When you look at something, you're not actually seeing the image directly. Your eyes only identify light beams. The eyes absorb the light beams into the back of the eye where something called rods (which see light/dark) and cones (which identify color) organize the light beams and then reflect them back toward the front of the eye where the retina is. The retina functions like a mirror; it takes the light beams from the rods and cones to form an image. This means that when you are "seeing" something with your physical eyes, what you are really "seeing" is a mirrored image from your own retinas. You're not seeing the actual image you were looking at, but a copy. There are an estimated 7-10 million cones and 800-1000 million rods! Your eyes work very hard to give you visual images of the world around you.

The sixth chakra also deals with visual images and it too translates light beams into visuals. The sixth chakra perceives and understands images from the moment of birth, but until a baby's brain is more advanced, the baby's mind cannot understand what it is seeing. When babies are first born, they do not see images with their physical eyes, they only see shades of light and dark. The eyes are directly connected to the brain and they "learn" to see as a baby gets older. The physical eyes are always forming an image against the retina; it's just that the brain needs to learn what that image is. It usually does this by association. A cup is held up to the baby and someone says "this is a cup," now the brain connects the defined item with the image it is getting. Even as an adult, your mind is still learning from your eyes. If you did not know what a kiwi was, and someone held the fruit in front of you, you would not be able to identify it. When you're an adult, you have enough brain function to say "I don't know what that is." As soon as you were educated as to what a kiwi was, your mind would then be able to translate and comprehend the image should you ever see a kiwi again. This is part of the human growth process. Your eyes see everything, but it is up to you as to how consciously aware you are, so it's up to you how much you acknowledge that which your eyes are already seeing.

This is the chakra that is probably most affected by a person's Defense System because the defenses are always trying to block the reality of what's really going on. For example, a person could have a close friend with anorexia. This friend has gone from 145 lbs. to 87 lbs. and has a very gaunt, sickly appearance. If the person does not want to face their friend's disease, they simply will not see it. Even though the person's physical appearance has changed drastically, they will see the same image that they have always seen. Eyesight problems come from this chakra. Glaucoma, which involves a gradual loss in eyesight, is now estimated to affect at least 60% of people over 65 years old. Energetically this comes from a persistent lifetime of not seeing Truth. All of the characterologies in the Defense System have an affect on this chakra. They all block it in some way.

This is the area where people distort their own image as well as everything around them. It is not uncommon for brain tumors to be linked to this chakra. Brain tumors are often related to energetic congestion inside the brain. The sixth chakra is always reflecting the Truth of what's really going on, so when a person is not seeing the Truth in a situation, the energy becomes clogged in the brain and can eventually cause a tumor.

The sixth chakra is most famous for being considered the "psychic" chakra. It is in the sixth dimension that all things are possible to be imagined and seen. This dimension deals a lot with alternate realities, alternate futures and distortions in time. By the last one I mean that the sixth dimension functions outside of what Mankind considers to be "time." It does not work directly on creation but rather on seeing endless possibilities from endless possible angles. The sixth dimension is very still. It's as if a person took 1000 photographs and laid all 1000 pictures down on the floor at the same time to look at. In the sixth dimension, you are able to just stand there and see all of those pictures *and* process trillions of pieces of information about them all in the same moment in time. In the other six dimensions (of the seven this book is addressing) you would have to look at each of the photos one at a time.

When someone is using this dimension for psychic ability, they are usually using it to see into other people's Energy Fields. This can give them information from everything to physical ailments, emotional issues, future issues and past issues. Because the sixth dimension does not function in a time zone, once a person can get their consciousness in the present, it is easy to see past and future. But remember, every day is created from this moment, and there is no such thing as a sure thing. Everyone's future is created by what they do today, so if you get a psychic reading about the future, that reading can change tomorrow.

In regards to psychic ability, the biggest problem with this chakra is abuse. A person can learn to be more aware of their sixth chakra, and some people are born already using their sixth chakra. *It does not mean that they are in the sixth dimension.* Because this planet is in the third dimension, most people who are using their psychic ability are using it from the third dimension. This can be a bit like giving a 5-year-old a power drill. Are they really ready to use it without supervision? When you enter the sixth chakra from the third dimension, it is so easy to use the gifts of this chakra to give your defenses more power, to psychically manipulate and control other people, to intimidate other people and to feed the Idealized Self-Image. A healthy psychic is a humble psychic, and a healthy psychic is one who does personal growth and self-healing work.

To work with the sixth chakra is to work with all that you deny. It takes a strong intention to see and seek the Truth because the Truth is not always pretty. If Truth was pretty, you probably wouldn't be in denial of it.

SEVENTH CHAKRA

This is the foundation for spiritual support in the physical body. This is also the place that the Magician considers to be a direct enemy.

It is at this level in the Chakra System that the Core Essence enters into the physical body.

The seventh chakra is responsible for the brain, the endocrine system and the skeletal system. It is inside your bones that bone marrow is created. Bone marrow is the source of all physical life as it is the source of your blood cells. It is your Essence that creates and continuously feeds the bone marrow. Degenerative bone diseases like osteoporosis and arthritis develop as a physical by-product of the lack of spiritual connection. Both diseases are progressive, showing that the body will literally crumble without spiritual support.

Brain tumors also develop when this chakra is not allowed to bring forth God's light. More commonly, psychiatric disorders and progressive brain deteriorative diseases like Parkinson's, Organic Brain Syndrome, Multiple Sclerosis, strokes and Alzheimer's are some of the physical results from the lack of connection between a person's brain and their seventh chakra.

This chakra is also referred to as the *crown* chakra and is often depicted in religious pictures as a golden halo or a white light surrounding the head of someone who has performed great spiritual acts.

It is at this dimensional level that God is no longer a concept but a reality, and the soul is no longer seen as something outside of the Self. A person can feel that they and their soul are one and the same. This chakra can be deeply affected by a person's upbringing. If spiritual or religious beliefs are forced on a child when growing up, or spiritual beliefs are denied when a child is growing up, this chakra can become distorted.

The seventh chakra is often used for channeling. Channeling is the process of connecting to the spiritual realms and communicating, or talking back and forth with spiritual energies from those realms. This may sound nice, but in reality a lot of harm can be done when a person is attempting to channel. Remember, just because an energy source is in a "spiritual realm" does not make it light. *Only to the degree that a person can connect to their own Core Essence and maintain a higher vibration of light for any length of time, can they connect to other spiritual energies that function from the light.* Otherwise, random channeling is no different than randomly picking out a house in the middle of Chicago and starting up a conversation with the owner. You don't know who that person really is or how "spiritually" based they are. My advice would be to start by channeling your own Higher Self or your own spiritual guide. Everyone has one. Start by getting to know yourself first, then go on. You have all of your own answers; it's just a matter of connection and a desire to become empowered.

Power versus empowerment is probably the biggest issue that holds people back when working with this chakra. As much as a person's conscious mind wants to connect to their Higher Self, their Lower Self does not want to see this happen. The Lower Self functions from personal power, the Higher Self functions from empowerment. The more a person can let go of their Victim Consciousness and their False Image, the easier it is for them to connect to their Core Essence from this chakra. This is because the Shadow Self gets its power from outside of itself, and the seventh chakra is all about empowering a person from within by allowing the Core Essence light to enter into the physical body and connect to all seven chakras. To work with this chakra requires a desire to let go of the need to control and have power over others in order to let your Higher Self come in, because the Higher Self will not play power games, manipulate or control anything or anyone. Essence is based in love and creative energy, the Magician is based in power games and controlling. The crown chakra asks you to pick one or the other.

CHAPTER NINETEEN

The Energy Field

The Energy Field is also known as the *aura* and is comprised of seven layers. Just like the Chakra System, each layer has a unique job to do, but all seven layers function together as one unit. Each layer of the Energy Field corresponds to a chakra. The first layer is called the Etheric level and connects into the first chakra. The second layer is called the Emotional level and connects into the second chakra. The third layer is the Mental level, the fourth is the Astral, the fifth is the Etheric Template, the sixth is the Celestial and the seventh is the Ketheric Template.

The Energy Field is your blueprint for life. Whereas the Chakra System translates information between the physical world (your body) and the Energy Field, the Energy Field *processes* information from both the Chakra System and the Core Essence. What this means is that the Energy Field is more than just a translator; it actually shifts and changes itself according to the information it receives by imprinting the information inside one or more levels of the Field. This process of imprinting creates a template, or blueprint, that both your physical body and your Core Essence work from.

Like the example used previously in this book, the process of imprinting is similar to taking a picture. Let's say you're taking a picture of a lake. The "lake" would be the raw information in the physical world, the act of taking the picture (the image going inside the camera) represents the chakras receiving information, and the photograph itself is the "imprint" that winds up somewhere in your Energy Field. If your Energy Field were perfectly healthy, it would

not have any "photographs" stuck in it. The Energy Field in its natural state is neutral. It doesn't hold onto anything, everything flows through it. In their natural state the chakras function the same way; they're neutral. Your first chakra does not decide what is safe and what's not safe. *You* actually make those decisions. It's just a matter of what part of yourself you are listening to when you make a decision, your Core Essence or your Shadow Self which is filled with fear-based concepts. When *you* decide you don't feel safe, your first chakra simply responds accordingly. Your chakras just do as they are told. So does your Energy Field. **You make all of your own life decisions; your entire Energy System simply reflects those decisions.** So there is never anything "wrong" with a person's chakras or any part of their Energy Field. These areas simply reflect what they are told. This is the significance of becoming **aware,** because it is the part of you that is unaware that usually controls most of your Energy System. As the old saying goes, "don't blame the messenger" (chakras/Energy Field), instead, take responsibility for the message.

When there is a distortion in the Energy Field, it means that something actually gets stuck in the Field, changing the flow of energy in and out of the system. It's the difference between being at the lake and holding a picture of the lake. A picture is a moment frozen in time. Any picture in your Energy Field is frozen. Generally speaking, we only freeze bad memories and experiences. This is why people re-live negative patterns over and over again, because these patterns are stuck in their Energy Field. The Energy Field takes these negative patterns and projects them out into your life.

For example, let's say a girl is born into a family where the father hits the mother. Her chakras will take this raw information from the physical realm and send it into the Energy Field. On a soul level, this girl is learning about abuse between men and women, so the Core Essence sends back a message to the Energy Field to hold onto the experience of seeing her mother physically beaten by her father. As this little girl gets older and can identify herself as a female, she notices that her mother is female and her father is male. In this scenario she develops a belief that says, "If you love me, you'll hit me." This belief becomes an actual pattern in her Energy Field. The pattern can show up in more than one level of the Field, for example it can be in the Etheric level (which deals with the physical body) and the Emotional level (which deals with passion, sex and emotions) at the same time.

Now the little girl grows up and becomes a woman who frequently finds herself in abusive relationships with men. This is because her Energy Field takes the belief regarding abuse and reflects it outward to the world, like a neon sign, trying to attract someone who will act out her belief. This is how a person can be in an abusive relationship and their mind understands that they need to get out, but they can't seem to leave, or if they do, they just go on to another relationship that turns out just as abusive. Until the pattern is released from the Energy Field, the behavior will not change. In this case she will continue to connect with men who abuse.

I have had many clients show up for a healing requesting help in releasing a relationship pattern that they have identified. In the United States, I have noticed a lack of tolerance for people who stay in severely unhealthy relationships. These relationships shouldn't be tolerated, no abuse should, but often when an abused spouse/partner seeks social care or medical help, they are judged and attacked for not leaving their abuser. This causes even greater mental pain and shame for the person seeking help. On the other side of the fence, the police department and emergency rooms in this country alone see *millions* of abuse cases each year, and the vast majority of abused people choose to return to the abuser. If the average person does not understand the concept that people are surrounded by an Energy Field that acts like a magnet, attracting to it situations and people that reflect all of the negative beliefs and wounds a person has, all they have to go on is what they see. And what they see is that person "A" abuses person "B," and person "B" chooses to go back home with person "A." Developing a better understanding of how Man functions (this means accepting that a person is a lot more complicated than the mind alone understands) and having compassion is part of the answer to this epidemic problem.

Energy flows from the Core Essence into the Energy Field through the Chakra System and then through your physical body. This whole process is what creates your physical reality. Technically, it is the Energy Field that sends the "blueprint" through the Chakra

System, into the physical body and out to your life. So, your physical body and chakra system are the translators while your Energy Field is the dynamic aspect of your Being that solidifies the information from the Core Essence, as well as the chakras and your body.

Like the Chakra System, the Energy Field can be observed from different dimensions. Each level of the Energy Field has its own color and structure and looks different depending on which dimension you are coming from or looking at. In the third dimension, just like the chakras, the first level is red in color, the second is orange, the third is yellow, the fourth green, the fifth blue, the sixth indigo and the seventh is white. When studying the Energy Field you can learn to physically feel all seven layers with hands-on energy training. Each level has a unique feel to it. Every other layer is structured, with the layers in between being unstructured or "soft" layers. The first, third, and fifth layers are structured, the second, fourth and sixth layers are soft. The soft layers are held together by the structure of the layer above and below it. The seventh layer is both structured and soft. It holds itself together as well as the rest of the Energy Field.

ETHERIC LEVEL

This is the mirror for the physical level and it is striated, meaning that it's composed of linear energy lines. An Etheric form is like an outline, so all of the bones and organs are seen but in outline form, like when you look at an x-ray of the body.

So when you look at this level (from the third dimension), it's like seeing an x-ray of the whole body that is covered in glowing lines. This level of the Energy Field is also known as a person's Etheric Body. When you touch this layer of the Field, it feels semi-firm, like touching an inflated balloon. This is the layer that holds the foundation for the other six levels of the Field, so the healthier it is, the healthier the Energy Field is.

The Etheric level is the blueprint for your physical body. If a person is developing a disease, like a tumor, it will show up in this level first. And it will look very similar to what the disease looks like in the physical body. For example, if a person was developing a two-inch tumor in their right ovary; you would see a two-inch tumor in their Etheric right ovary. Before a person develops a physical illness, it will develop completely in the Etheric level first, often giving a person physical symptoms that will not show up on any medical testing.

An example of this would be an autoimmune disease, like Fibromyalgia. It usually takes many years before an autoimmune disease is formally diagnosed because a person will experience symptoms long before the physical body shows definitive changes. This means that a patient will have symptoms for years without conclusive test results or a conclusive diagnosis. Many patients go to their medical doctor with physical complaints of pain or other symptoms yet nothing shows up on physical exam or in their test results. Medically this can be frustrating and confusing for both the patient and the medical community. Energetically, this is because all disease develops very slowly. A disease has to first fill up a person's Etheric body before spilling over into their physical body. While a disease is in the process of becoming a medically diagnosed event, it is trying to get the person's attention by producing physical symptoms. Your Etheric body does not want you to get sick so it tries to send you messages that something is not right by sending you physical symptoms in hopes that you will look within to see what is going on.

Listen to your body. It knows more about what's going on than you do, and it's trying to get itself healed before things get worse. This is why a person develops aches and pains; the body is trying to tell you something. Your physical body is a great teacher, and it is your Etheric body that holds the lesson plan.

EMOTIONAL LEVEL

The second layer is the Emotional level, and like its name implies, it holds all of the energy that is used to form your emotions and your passions. This level of the Field is soft and playful. When touching it, it can feel like what you might imagine touching a cloud would be like. It is also very sensitive and will contract itself into a tight and fearful energy if it perceives that anyone is trying to use or harm it.

Emotional abuse is very common, and this layer of the Field is a gentle one, so it tends to get bruised if there is abuse. Any level of the

Energy Field can literally develop a bruise when injured. The soft layers of the Field are more prone to bruising than the structured layers. Structured layers are more prone to tearing than bruising.

When a person has a lot of emotional wounds, the Emotional level becomes very large due to all the "pictures" being held in this layer. This is a problem when the Etheric level is not at least equally (if not more) expanded than the Emotional level. This is because the Emotional layer of the Field is *supported* by the Etheric layer. If the Emotional level is large and the Etheric level is small, it's like asking a piece of tissue paper to hold up a full glass of water. Eventually, the tissue paper will break. This is often how physical disease occurs. Issues from the layers above the Etheric level, like the Emotional level, spill down into the Etheric level and eventually into the physical body causing illness.

Emotions are comprised of highly charged energy. There is a lot of passion and creativity at this level and the energy is very active. Each level of the Energy Field has the potential to hold the same amount of energetic particles, but the soft levels are more outwardly active whereas the structured levels use the energy to hold everything in place. It's like water in a glass. The "glass" represents the structured level and the "water" is the soft level. If the glass is not big enough or strong enough, it cannot hold a large amount of water flowing into it. When someone's emotions "take over," energetically this is very literal because the Emotional body loses its support and the energy spills outward.

It is not healthy for a person to work on having strong emotional releases until their structural foundation, the Etheric level, can handle it. Over the past decade there seems to be a fixation on "working with emotions" and expressing emotions through both healing work and traditional therapy. This is certainly a part of the work, but your Emotional aspect is just one level in your overall Being. And like all of life, it needs to be worked with in a balanced way. According to the Bible, Noah built his ark *before* the floods came, not after. It's very hard to deal with a flood of emotions if you haven't got a strong foundation to contain them. Without a strong foundation, the Emotional layer just winds up spilling out all over the Energy Field creating a strong Victim Consciousness.

MENTAL LEVEL

This is the next structured level and holds all the energy that is used in the decision/opinion making process. This is the area where random and collective thoughts are held. The Belief System has its strongest hold at this level. When feeling this level, it does not have the same solid strength as the first layer, but it does have a clear strength, like touching plexi-glass.

Unlike the Emotional level, which tends to get too bulky, this level can become too rigid, making it smaller than it should be. Rigid thoughts and narrow-mindedness lead to a small Mental level. The structured layers of the Field do not have the soft flow of the unstructured layers, but they are still flowing in their own way. The unstructured layers are more creative; they randomly throw lots of ideas and feelings out, so the energy itself is random. The structured layers have a more direct purpose; they take the randomly flowing energy and channel it into something solid like an action or a thought. At the Mental level, this energy is channeled into beliefs, opinions and thoughts.

This level is constrained when a person grows up in a constrained environment. Mainly this means an environment that is regimented or does not allow for personal opinions to be created, stated and honored.

This is the level that can become very dense by taking on other people's ideas, opinions and beliefs versus creating your own. When this level becomes dense, a person is more likely to spend their time in their Defense System. The Mental layer is all about forming originality and individuality. The less a person's consciousness is comfortable in their own individuality, the more defended they become. This layer of the Energy Field tends to lose a lot of its energy to either being in a defense or giving over to someone else's defense.

ASTRAL LEVEL

This is the first layer of the Field that holds energy for greater purpose. This does not mean that this level is "greater" than the first three levels; it just means that at this level your energy is now about a larger purpose versus a self-serving purpose.

The first three levels of the Energy Field focus on personal issues in the here and now. The Astral level is the first dimension that a person can enter to consciously explore other dimensions. This includes past and future existence. It is at this level that all individual experiences start to be seen as part of a larger experience. This is also the first level where the Core Essence is the prevailing energy. The first three levels allow more of the Shadow Self energy to be prevalent for the purpose of self-exploration. It is at this level that spiritual exploration becomes the focus.

The Astral level is a soft layer that holds comforting and loving energy. Specifically, this is where unconditional love from God is held. When feeling this layer, it can be like millions of bubbles floating around; some of the bubbles are in groups and others float gently by themselves. Each "bubble" encompasses the soul connection for *every* interaction a person has.

This layer is conscious of what is happening on both the dimensional levels of the Core Essence as well as the Shadow Self. In other words, it deals with the Higher Self and the Lower Self all at the same time. The Core Essence deals with group consciousness as well as individual consciousness, so it is at this level that a person's awareness extends beyond the Self and understands that in some way, we are all connected. For example, if two people are having a general conversation over lunch, at this level they would be aware of how each other is being affected by the conversation on multiple dimensions.

Compassion and understanding are the key elements floating around the Astral level. These elements can be hard to find if someone enters this level from an unenlightened place. This is easy to do if you seek spiritual enlightenment but are not willing to look at your own darkness. Often people use this layer with a low level of awareness, meaning that their consciousness is attached only to what they want to see. When this happens, it's easy to increase the amount of energy in a person's Shadow Self because their Magician becomes exposed to unconditional love but *they* have yet to become unconditionally loving. There is a huge difference. The Magician then learns how to *appear* loving, for example, do what would be considered a "loving act" but for manipulative reasons, fooling the person's consciousness into believing that they are "enlightened" and "loving" when, in fact, they are not.

The loving and spiritually connected energy in the Astral level is there for all. The more a person is willing to work through their Shadow Self, the more they *become* loving and spiritually connected, allowing for full use of the energy found in the Astral level.

ETHERIC TEMPLATE

This level holds all of the energy used to create the blueprint for the physical world. It is the precursor to the first layer in the Field, the Etheric level. It is at this level that outward creation, or manifestation, happens. The Etheric Template is the layer in the Energy Field that projects energy outward to manifest a person's physical reality. This includes all that is in your physical world as well as your physical body. So actually, all physical disease starts here before going to your Etheric level and then on down to the physical body.

This level doesn't just work on illness; it works on *everything* you create including what you want to speak out. For example, you can think "I want a pizza," but until you order the pizza or get up and make the pizza, you don't actually get the pizza! Manifestation requires that you have an idea or a thought about something, and then add enough passion and desire to make it happen. It is at this level that a person makes desire and thought a reality not by force, but rather creation. Your internal desires create your external reality. The Etheric Template is filled with *creator* energy. Notice, I did not say "creative" because creative energy comes from the Emotional level; it is the manifesting of that creative energy that happens here. The Emotional level uses its passion to come up with a creative idea or desire, and the Etheric Template uses its power of creation to make it happen. You can think of the Emotional level as internalized creative energy and the Etheric Template as external creation. This level makes something happen, or not happen, in real life by the process of manifestation. It takes personal creative desire and forms a physical creation. Not doing something is also a creation; it is the creation of inaction which takes a lot of work because our natural state is to create action.

The Astral level requires communication to work. You have to say what you want or it won't happen. External creation requires movement of some kind, whether it is your voice saying "I'll take that one" or your own physical body moving. Either way, a person has to actively participate at this level. Not participating causes this level to become blocked. This is probably the most common reason people have difficulty manifesting what they want; they either don't act on what they want (usually it is a simple case of not speaking out their needs, like "hey, stop the car because I have to go!") or they don't have enough desire/intention behind what they want. It takes a lot of free flowing energy to be able to manifest. The more someone's energy is tied up in their Shadow Self, the less energy they have to create because they are using their energy to cycle and maintain a False Self instead of allowing it to flow freely. The more a person is coming from their Core Essence, the faster their thoughts become reality. As you can imagine, it could be very detrimental for a person, and the planet, if everyone just manifested what they thought! Look at how many negative or harmful thoughts you have in just thirty minutes. At times, a sluggish and slow-manifesting Etheric Template is really God's savior.

CELESTIAL LEVEL

This layer contains the energy used for spiritual insight. It is in this level that a person can see and experience themselves as part of the Celestial environment. In the Astral level a person can begin to understand the spiritual levels, but it is in the Celestial level that a person can *feel* the spiritual realms. It's no longer a concept but a reality.

The Celestial level is where spiritual guides can have a great influence on souls. This level is where a soul examines their purpose, their past and what they would like to explore. The spiritual guides that work from this level are known as *guardians* and become the mentor for each soul they work with, helping them to grow towards having conscious awareness that they are one with God. There are guides in the lower dimensions and their job is to help a person grow and learn from the individuated Self and their individualized experiences. At this level, a guide is exchanged for a guardian. You can think of it as exchanging a high school level teacher for a college professor.

Again, one is not better than the other; they are simply at different levels of evolution.

The Celestial level is where the in-depth spiritual work is done. From the perspective of someone in the first five dimensions, this level helps them to see the bigger picture and how their decisions and experiences affect everyone. From the perspective of the sixth dimension, this is where a soul begins to let go of its concept of separation from God.

KETHERIC TEMPLATE

This level holds the energy that is specific to each person's direct connection to their soul. It is the level where the soul creates the template for a person's lifetime. This layer is both structured and soft. The structured energy holds all seven layers of the Field together. The soft energy feeds information to all seven layers of the Field. As the Etheric Template level is the blueprint for the Etheric level (and your physical body), the Ketheric Template level is the blueprint for the entire Energy Field.

A blueprint is simply a design structure. This level holds the design, or the structure, for all a soul is going to need in a particular lifetime. What fills the structure is your experiences and your choices. So whether you allow your structure to be filled with your Core Essence or your Shadow Self has a lot to do with your conscious choices. And your conscious choices have everything to do with how you perceive and react to each and every experience you have in life.

A person's Ketheric Template influences their lifetime by what it does, and does not, add to their blueprint. For example, a person may have minimal to no musical ability in their Ketheric Template. As a soul, this person may be very musically inclined but during this particular lifetime the soul will not add this innate skill to their Template because the soul wants to grow in other areas. So this person may love and appreciate music but be unable to play a note! They're not meant to actively participate in music during this lifetime. On the other end of the spectrum, a soul may add all accumulated knowledge from all previous experiences into this Template to create a lifetime where they put it all together. It would be like someone going through years of medical school and residency then finally getting to a place in their life where all the information and learning comes together and they become a great surgeon. At the Template level, it's about lifetimes of information coming together.

This is the level where a soul weaves together all of its experiences into a tapestry that becomes the Template for their lifetime. During the lifetime, a person will add to, and change, the threads that are already woven into the tapestry, forever changing and re-weaving their existence.

Life is a Mirror

CHAPTER TWENTY

Life Is a Mirror

Everything around you is a mirror—people, places and objects. They all reflect what is being projected from your Energy Field every day. Both your Shadow Self and your Core Essence are shining outward from your Field, but it's the information in the Shadow that makes life sad, hard, painful and dark. For example, when a person has a Shadow-based issue, like a prejudice, that prejudice will keep coming back to haunt them until it is dealt with. If you're prejudiced against "red," it will show up in your life everywhere. People standing next to you will be wearing red, you're stuck in an elevator with people wearing red, you go out to your car in the parking lot and all of the cars surrounding it are red. "Red" will be in your face, irritating you until the day you stop and look at what issues, beliefs or wounds you have surrounding it. All of life is a mirror reflecting what is really going on inside of you. Energy Healing involves stopping and looking at the patterns around you. What is being mirrored back to you today?

Energy Healing is the art of intuitively helping a client acknowledge their Shadow Self and their Core Essence. This is frequently done by helping people to acknowledge their mirrors. People often victimize themselves by projecting their issues onto other people or use other people's successes to confirm a distorted belief in themselves that they can never be successful, smart, rich, happy etc. Either way, they are not taking responsibility for the fact that the other person, group or situation is merely reflecting their own Self back to them.

All of life is a mirror. This does not mean that everything is as literal as it appears to be on the surface. For example, you could be standing in front of someone who is yelling. They could even be yelling directly at you. This does not mean that they are mirroring your own repressed anger back at you. They could be mirroring an issue you have about not being comfortable with raw emotions, or an issue of how you cave in when someone yells at you, and your Higher Self is just trying to help you see that you need to strengthen your boundaries. The possibilities are endless as to what the mirror is actually showing you.

How do you know what is being mirrored back to you? The more you become consciously aware of your Core Essence, the more your intuition will develop. It is your intuitive skills that assist you in understanding yourself, including understanding your mirrors. It is your intuition that helps you to discern what *your* stuff is versus the other person's stuff. When someone is mirroring something to you, it is rarely 50-50, so it's your intuition that will help you to own what percent is yours and let go of the rest. Intuitive skills become clearer and clearer the more connected you become to your Core Essence.

If you look at the concept 'that life is a mirror' and take this knowledge out into the world with just your mind, you can end up analyzing everything and everyone around you. This will not help you to become more enlightened, and it will actually increase the energy in your Defense System. Your defenses love to be analytical as a way to avoid the link of intuitive connection to your Higher Self.

One thing you can do is relax and just look at the overall patterns that go on around you instead of trying to analyze everything that happens in a day. Your overall patterns will lead you into further understanding of where you have a strong connection to your Core Essence and where you are connected to your Shadow Self.

Seeing a professional healer is another way to explore and work with your patterns, your spiritual connection, and releasing that which you hold onto in unhealthy ways. Things really do "weigh you down," literally, because your issues and wounds hang on to your Energy Field re-creating themselves every day. Energy Healing is based on the concept of shifting your whole being by working with both the Shadow Self and Core Essence, not just reacting and fixing life's problems. Life's "problems" are soul issues. These issues will follow you through time and keep you from connecting to your True Self until the patterns behind the issues are resolved.

LOOKING FOR A GOOD HEALER?
HERE'S A FEW THINGS TO KNOW BEFORE TAKING
THE PLUNGE....

CHAPTER TWENTY-ONE

Choosing Your Healer

The relationship between client and healer is a very personal one. Like any decision in life, it's important to make it with as much awareness as possible. The first step is to listen to your intuition. Ask your Higher Self to connect you to the best possible healer for you at this time.

When you feel guided towards a particular healer, set up an appointment. Follow through with that appointment. This may seem like a silly statement, but often when a healer is a good match with what your Higher Self has in mind for you, your Lower Self will become fearful and distrustful (as it knows it is about to get broken down). The Lower Self can come up with all kinds of clever ways to keep you from keeping the appointment. Remember, your Lower Self likes to stay in its victim role so it does not want you to increase your connection to your Higher Self, let alone your Higher Purpose.

Sometimes the more anxious a person feels prior to going to a healer can be an indication that the healer is just what the Higher Self ordered! Other times that anxiety can be telling you that this is not a good match. How to tell the difference? An effective healing session will often leave you with the feeling of being "connected" during and after the session. You may not always feel comfortable or complete after a session, but if you feel within yourself and are honest with yourself, an effective healing session will leave you feeling more connected to yourself, your life and everything around you because you will have more *awareness*.

An example of this is John S. who goes for a healing session because he is having difficulty at work with his boss. During this particular session he discovers that his boss is reflecting back to him how he truly feels about his wife and his marriage. The realization comes out that he has a desire to leave his wife of ten years and has displaced his anger about the situation towards his boss. On one level, John S. may leave the session feeling very agitated because of all the raw emotion and Truths that were discovered. On another level, he will feel more connected to himself and his life. He will have more awareness. The more awareness we have in life is directly related to how healthy and clear our decision-making process is.

You may feel very anxious when you first meet your healer to begin a session. If the relationship is a good match, when the session is over you will feel more comfortable with the healer. Also, it's not uncommon that at the end of the session there is a feeling of "coming home" or that this particular healer really understood you. Really saw deep inside of you. These are some examples of what it's like to find a good match between healer and client. An example of a poor match is when you feel anxious, fearful, or maybe even a sense that you were being controlled, attacked, judged or manipulated by the healer.

If you have already experienced your initial healing session and think that you would like to see this particular healer on a regular basis, it's time to start asking a few questions. *You have every right.* If you are choosing a medical doctor, a lawyer, a therapist or an accountant, it's a good idea to take the time to find out a little about them, like what their credentials are for example, or their ethics. Personally, I want to know if my accountant thinks that "a little cheating" is okay at tax time. I want to make sure our ethics match before I contract out their service. This should be no different when choosing a healer.

When a healer and a client see each other on a committed, regular basis, the healer is agreeing to take on the role of spiritual teacher. It's not that they are there to teach you about your spirit, but rather to help guide you to find your own spirit and spiritual answers. This is a very serious relationship.

A healthy healer usually has some credentials behind them, although this can certainly be well argued, as Jesus Christ, Buddha and the Dalai Lama have no formal "degree" they can whip out and show you in regards to spiritual training. But these are examples of spiritual Masters, and in their respective lifetimes, they did study the art of spirituality, each in their own way. I do know that every good teacher is also a student. Ask your healer about their background in healing and spirituality including any formal training they may have in the Healing Arts. What gives them the right to hang out the proverbial "shingle" that says they're a healer? What have they studied? What is their philosophy?

This is not to be naïve. A degree, certificate or some well-known teacher does not assure any kind of competency. I have met many a person with a handful of fancy degrees and yet they are clearly incompetent in their job. This is where your intuition will help. The best advice I can give is that every good healer has a good healer, every good teacher has a good teacher, and very often a healthy healing practice has another healer supervising that practice. This is a basic checks-and-balance system. It's easy for anyone to get caught up in their Shadow Self and start playing God instead of coming from a place that is connected to God. Healing is a vocation that directly affects so many lives on such a deep and serious level. It's not a job to be taken lightly, so don't take your role as a healing client or a healing student lightly either. Your healer has their responsibilities and you have yours. Part of your responsibility is in asking questions and making sure that you are comfortable with the healer.

At this time in the United States, Energy Healing is quickly becoming vogue. Be cautious of this. I have met many a "healer" without any formal training doing more harm than good on a daily basis in their practice. This is not to say there aren't some really great healers out there practicing without any formal training. There probably are. I just haven't met one. To be fair I've also met many healers *with* formal training doing a great deal of harm in their practice, but by far, in my experience the former out weighs the latter, a lot.

It's easy for a healer to profess being "great" to a client. Or for that matter practicing the art of healing in a room full of people who have nothing to compare it to because, if the audience is not intuitive, they won't know if what the healer is claiming to be "truth" really is the

Truth. It's another thing altogether for a healer to stand in front of a group of their peers and allow their healing skills to be observed. Formal training should **require** this of a healer. Just like any licensed therapist, a formally trained healer should have spent a percentage of their training in supervised practice sessions complete with feedback from their supervisor. No formally trained and licensed surgeon gets to cut into a patient without first having years of supervised surgery. A healer should be no different. After all, they are potentially cutting into *your* Energy Field. So, one of the first things to look for in a healer is what kind of formal training they have had. Formal training is not defined as a weekend course or even a week course in some kind of healing seminar. Formal training is long term and on-going.

Something that can indicate a healer may not be in a healthy place is that they want something from you. This is not about normal financial compensation. A client normally exchanges money with their healer as a way of contracting services. No, this is something deeper. A healer is not in a healthy place if their *intention* for the healing is financial gain, if they want you to "spread the word" about them, or they want you to join some organization that they are a part of. If they want you to give them feedback as to how they are doing (that's what they're supposed to be getting supervision for!), or if they want to please you, control you or have you obey them. Be careful if they're keeping some kind of written or unwritten progress report on your sessions. *A healing session is not psychotherapy.* It is a session of exploration, discovery and the shifting of energy from the Shadow Self back to the Core Essence. It's not about "getting some place" but rather about learning to increase awareness in the moment and learning to just Be. So if either you or your healer are keeping some kind of progress report that has anything to do with where you "should be," this is not healthy. To have a goal is part of setting an intention for the session. A progress report is judgment.

A healer is not in a healthy place if they want you to depend on them. A client will often go through periods when they feel needy or dependent on their healer. It is the responsibility of the healer **not** to foster these feelings, but rather guide the client towards self-realization of their own empowerment.

Everyone is constantly going through transitions, even your healer, so, knowing this, take some time to test out the relationship. You truly do learn something every day. It may not always be pleasant or enjoyable, but you do go to sleep with more experience than when you woke up. Even if the relationship between you and your healer winds up not being for you, take stock of what you learned about your Self in that relationship and use the knowledge for the next one.

Sometimes you know after just a few sessions that the relationship either is, or is not going to work. A person may spend as much as a year with the same healer but then decide to move on. Even if it doesn't work out, it's not as if the relationship was necessarily a poor match for the whole year. You might simply have outgrown that particular healer, or the healer changed towards an area that's not for you.

If you have gone through two to three healers in a short period of time, then you need to pick one healer/client relationship and stick it out for a few months. (This can mean at least four months.) You may need to realize that the "problem" is with you, not the healer. Two common ways people deal with something inside themselves that they don't really want to face is avoidance and blame. They avoid finding a good healer and blame everyone that they do find. **Be aware that projecting your own issues onto your healer is the most common thing people do.** A client may leave a session saying something like "That healer wasn't listening to me" or "Oh, that healer has some serious issues of their own!" when in fact it was the client that was not listening to the healer because they didn't like what the healer had to say—even though what the healer had to say was completely True. And the healer was not expressing their own issues, but reflecting back to the client issues that the client was not seeing for themself at the time of the healing.

For any healing to be truly effective, as the client you have to have a strong intention to see, hear and acknowledge things about yourself that in all likelihood are not attractive traits when initially seen. It is the exploration of these traits that will bring you closer to your Core Essence and more aware of your Shadow Self. This is what will change your life, and lifestyle, on a permanent basis. No quick, temporary fixes here. But you have to be willing to face yourself for these changes to come about.

The fact is, sometimes you may worship your healer, and sometimes you may hate your healer. Sometimes you will believe in them, and sometimes you might not. But in the end, any healthy relationship will have mutual respect.

One more note. Remember, your healer is not your God or your path to God. Only you are your own path and only you will know *your* True God. A healer is there to help guide you when you start to wander off your path, to remind you to look down on a regular basis so you can see the cracks in the road, to check and make sure that you are indeed on *your* path and not caught up in someone else's. And probably one of the most important things is to help you have the courage to look down towards your path, then back up to your heart, and honor yourself for the courage you have in daring to open your eyes as you walk through this world.

About the Author

Susan D. Matz came into the world with strong gifts of healing, intuition and a conscious connection to her Higher Purpose. This ability to be so aware of her purpose in the world has been a strong motivating factor in helping others remember their purpose. After twelve years of working as an ER/ICU trauma nurse, Susan left the field of traditional medicine and opened her own healing practice. She has spent years studying religion, spiritual philosophies and Energy Healing. Susan has a private healing practice in Chicago and is the founder/director of the A'claire School for Healing. You can contact Susan at info@aclaire.com

"Between the covers of this book is the chance to discover the road to self-awareness. Open your heart and be willing to see yourself as you really are. The journey is amazing."

—Anita Lara

"One of the truly revolutionary concepts in Susan's book is that we create everything in our lives. WE are responsible for everything in our hearts and minds, for the consequence of our actions, and even for the things that "happen" to us. This allows a tremendous shift away from external blame to experiencing every second of our lives as filled with becoming and the opportunity to learn something new about ourselves. Life, in this sense, is a learning tool."

—David Kopaez, M.D.

"Susan has helped me gain understanding, insight and awareness as to why my life is the way it is and the tools to change it if I choose to do so."

—Christine Lega

"Susan's work taught me to go into myself and find the origin points for many of my distorted perceptions. From here, I'd been unconsciously creating the same negative experiences. I learned to bring my conscious awareness there, and enormous patterns woven into my being were able to shift and transmute back into their undistorted 'true' vibration. This process brought me freedom from a terrible emptiness I had carried inside me all my life."

—Lisa Rogers

"Susan showed me that my own defenses had me trapped in a self-defeating cycle, but one that I could choose to step out of. Applying Susan's teaching to my life has helped me make a profound shift."

—Elena Arrigo

"*The Art of Energy Healing* has helped me to understand why and how I have created my life. It gave me the technical information to understand the patterns in my life, and it challenged me to go deeper in my own process of self-discovery."

—Melanie Traxler

"*The Art of Energy Healing* is a gift of love. It presents simple concepts with a tremendous amount of depth; it is a profound foundation for expansion into True Self."

—Mary Pat Traxler, Ph.D.

"Through Susan Matz and her teachings, I have learned and experienced that the answers and my unique purpose come from within. This work has enabled me to become more greatly aware of myself and all that is around me—to understand depth and connection. The movement and progression in my life is expansive and incredibly gratifying. There has been no greater gift in my life than to have met Susan Matz and to have the privilege of being one of her students."

—Karen Andre

"What I like about Susan's books is that they are easy to read without a lot of technical terms, and the information is presented in a neutral way. There are plenty of 'real world' examples that helped me to apply what I was reading to my life."

—Kathy Tullio

"Susan has a gift for explaining the complicated human Energy System in simple terms that makes it easy to understand. Reading her books is a profound experience."

—Julie Wagner

"Susan's profound connection and understanding of the human soul goes beyond anything I have ever known."

—Cheri Davis

"Susan has opened her heart to all of humanity and explained in great depth what makes us who we are and what the process of Energy Healing truly is. I know I have only scratched the surface of my journey, but my passion has been ignited and I am ready and excited to experience the next level."

—Jillian Payne

"Most of my time was spent in great pain, flailing around and blaming others for my misfortunes. From Susan and her sincere knowledge of human energies and how we fuel ourselves, I've developed a deeper understanding and acceptance of who I am and how I affect others.."

—Elizabeth Treger

"*The Art of Energy Healing* is a Rough Guide for the journey inward. Written with a simple clarity, Susan describes the layers of personality and the obstacles to self-awareness. She doesn't tell you where you will end up, but rather points out what you are likely to see along the way. And, most importantly, she places self-love and self-acceptance at the center of this journey."

—Samuel Smucker

"How can the Knower become the Known? This question puzzled the ancient Hindu mystics and philosophers. Susan's book provides a framework with which to pursue this quest of Self-Awareness. This is not a book of answers—it is made clear that the place to look is within—rather the book provides a method and conceptual framework that can be used to understand one's Self. Susan outlines the various conscious and unconscious parts of the Self, including Light elements of the Higher Self and Guide, and Dark elements of the Shadow and energetic defenses, and the Center, which encompasses both."

—David Kopaez, M.D.

"Susan encourages people to learn who they are and why they do the things they do by explaining the Energy System. It has helped me to understand myself more and in my practice."

—Julie Wagner, Energy Healer

Printed in the United States
40448LVS00007B/133-159

9 781577 331452